FOR THE LOVE OF THE GUN

G000269230

FOR THE LOVE OF THE GUN

'HE PUT HIS HANDS UP, PLEADING FOR HIS LIFE: DON'T KILL ME. PLEASE DON'T KILL ME.'

VIC DARK

JOHN BLAKE

Published by John Blake Publishing Ltd,
3, Bramber Court, 2 Bramber Road,
London W14 9PB, England

www.blake.co.uk

First published in paperback in 2006

ISBN 1 84454 196 7

British Library Cataloguing-in-Publication Data:

A catalogue record for this book is available from the British Library.

Design by www.envydesign.co.uk

Printed in Great Britain by Bookmarque

1 3 5 7 9 10 8 6 4 2

Papers used by John Blake Publishing are natural, recyclable products made
from wood grown in sustainable forests. The manufacturing processes conform
to the environmental regulations of the country of origin.

Every attempt has been made to contact the relevant copyright-holders,
but some were unobtainable. We would be grateful if the appropriate people
could contact us.

DEDICATION
For Sam, my kids and my friends.

'VIC DARK AND I BECAME
FRIENDS. HE HAD EARNED THE
RESPECT OF MANY PEOPLE.'
REG KRAY, 2000

CONTENTS

PROLOGUE: FOOTSTEPS IN THE DARK

'I HAVE ALWAYS FELT THAT IF THAT
BIG BASTARD HAD NOT RUN SO HARD
AT ME AS I WAS PLUNGING THE KNIFE
INTO HIM HE WOULD NOT HAVE LOST
HIS SPLEEN. IT POPPED RIGHT OUT.'

VICTOR DARK, 2003

I was buried alive. The cozzer was standing above me and I had two guns pointing at his nuts which I swear I could hear clicking like castanets.

And he didn't even know I had bullets ready to blast away his bollocks and the rest of his lunch box. He just knew he was hunting this hard, tearaway gunman who had been put on armed and highly dangerous alert. He was searching for a horrible, mad bastard who would shoot to kill. A right fucker who thought he was Rambo.

That was me. And it was spot on. I was totally tooled up and ready to rock and roll. At that point I was willing to shoot my way out of trouble. I didn't see an alternative. I had been a very bad bastard that night. Now it was smash or mash, and even in the hazards of the moment that thought made me smile.

I had buried myself in a potato field to escape the scores of armed police who were after me. I lay as still as I could in the spuds and mud. For a time, I felt like Houdini – as though I could get out of anything. I pictured Steve McQueen in his best movie *The Getaway* when, just by strength and character, fucking serious willpower – and a giant of a shotgun – he gets and takes what he wants and escapes. They have happy endings in the movies, even for bad boys. My fantasy world didn't last long. All too soon the dream vanished, fast, like a blind being snapped shut, and the pages of a real-life horror story started turning. And I became Britain's nightmare.

I had been eating dirt for eight hours when the police patrols got near.

Shittingly, this cozzer stood on my leg. I froze. I was certain he could hear the adrenalin banging around my body like a bad drug. I could. I didn't know whether to stay buried alive or go out rucking and shooting off my two snub-nosed .38 revolvers. I wouldn't have survived. And neither would many of them.

First, I had to decide whether to blast this cozzer's bollocks off or stay hidden – that man is a father today so you know my decision. It also kept me alive. Yet, I still don't understand how I could think so clearly. It had been an interesting evening even for a professional armed robber. Whatever daredevil games we played, blaggers like me tried to avoid taking hostages and hijacking cars.

Especially taking a cozzer along for a 100mph ride. With a Chinese takeaway.

I had shot a nightclub manager. My mate had been shot. So, to get us away, to save my so-called friend, I kidnapped a cozzer, an Irishman in his underpants and a Chinaman. Instead of the prawn fried rice and sweet and sour chicken (and extra helpings of that hot chilli dipping sauce 'cos I like a bit of fire in the belly) included in my takeaway that night was the Chinaman's car.

The cozzer was terrified but I told him I wasn't going to kill him and then he drove his hijacked Panda car over a bump and the gun which I had cosily tucked in next to his head went off. The bullet all but nicked his ear and I shouted: 'Sorry, I didn't mean to do that.' He went a little pale.

There you have it. An evening out for professional armed robber Vic Dark with his bullet-ridden mate, the cozzer, the Irishman and the Chinaman. And half of the Old Bill in London. All armed to the teeth.

But shit happens. I knew that after I left school. I was already a gangster graduate when, at 19 years old, I chopped up a body.

I had found early on in my life that I could bring terror to places and to people. It is an extravagant talent. Let me tell you about it.

But fasten your seat belt.

It's going to be a bumpy ride.

CHAPTER ONE

YOUNG GUNS

'I ALWAYS WANTED THINGS TO GO
QUIETLY. BUT I WAS ALWAYS PREPARED
TO KILL AND BE KILLED.'

VICTOR DARK, 2003

By choice, I was a professional armed robber so I went to work with guns. Not a briefcase, but a gun. Sometimes several guns. Shotguns. Revolvers. Pistols. Weapons of terror were part of my trade. I could do damage with my feet and my fists, with my head – I quite fancy myself with my head because of my instant reactions – but waving a big piece of hardware in front of a bank clerk or an enemy gets their attention faster than anything. Unless they think they are going to get a nasty stripe with a big, sharp Stanley knife.

You can shout, 'Get down, mother-fucker' as much as you like but unless they think they might be dead within a second, where's the intimidation? I always wanted things to go quietly. But I was always prepared to kill and be killed. That's part of the armed robbery business. It's only the druggies and the crazies, the mad cunts, who don't understand that. That's society's problem in the 21st century – the druggies and the crazies. Their disease provokes mayhem.

Armed robbery is a business. It takes time, brains, nerve and, though I say it myself, some style and class. Armed robbers? We're the Frank Sinatra of villains: smooth, cool and always in tune with the moment. I find that ramming a sawn-off shotgun in some wally's left ear is the perfect recipe for getting things My Way. You don't want to pull the trigger but you must always be willing to blast someone's face off or put them in a wheelchair for the rest of their lives. The punter always knows when you will do it. As I wrote earlier, terror is a talent. It's like the alphabet: you learn it and you never forget it.

I still know my ABCs.

They're robbing in the City of London and Wall Street every day. I just did it with a gun – and never made a ten-million-pound bonus. I was an honest gunman. I never lied about my trade. I have always kept to my personal principles, to my honour. I paid for that by giving Her Majesty lots of my time, lots of my pleasure, in some of Britain's toughest prisons.

I have problems with the system but it never got the better of me. I fought it all the way and that is what kept me sane and safe inside the atrociously run UK penal system. I took the kickings and the mental torment but I survived, sometimes with emotional difficulty, to be a seriously stronger man. I'll tell you tales of Britain's jails which will stop you driving at more than 30mph. You don't want any of it. Inside, it is a constant Mexican stand-off. Few really know who the bad guys are.

Of course, I do. I was a bad guy from the start. I always wanted maximum firepower, to be totally tooled up. You sure that seat belt's fastened?

My first gun was a .410 shotgun. It was a single barrel and very old-fashioned. You had to pull the hammers back. Imagine a crossbow. I bought it from a strange gypsy who used to hang around the pubs in Stratford in east London. I paid a hundred quid for it, which was a lot of cash in 1972 when I was 17 years old. But I knew from the start that I had to be armed – and that you have to jump in. One barrel put me in the armed robbery business. The gypsy was one of those who talked about black magic and he had a woman with him who sold flowers. Sold herself as well but I didn't fancy any of her. It was bad enough dealing with her garlic-whiffing old man. It was liked doing a deal with the devil and, I suppose, the way things turned out, it was.

If you read the books, Faustian is what they call that sort of deal. Bollocks. I wanted the gun to get what I desired. I'd used my wits and fists long enough. I needed firepower, for what I really wanted was the world. I may have aimed my gun sights low now and again, at kneecaps and lunch boxes, but not my ambitions and expectations. I never did and I never have. I wanted the top of the world. I learned my profession.

If you were trying to take the engine block out of a car what gun would you use? A .45 with dum-dum bullets would crack the engine block – the bullets would bang straight through the radiator and blow the block up. That handgun could stop a car and it's easy to handle and conceal, not like some great fucking artillery gun. If you are going to be a professional you need to be scientific, not slapdash. I know what gun is capable of what. Throughout my career as an armed robber my concern was always what each individual I worked with was capable of. Guns you could trust 99 per cent of the time. People? I wouldn't give you odds.

The more money I got, the more I went up in firepower: it made sense reinvesting the profits back into the business. Double-barrel shotguns, which I cut down to sawn-offs, were a favourite. They were black or dull silver, nickel plated. A lot of them were out of farmhouses. Some of them early ones were fucking lovely. It seemed a shame to cut them down but that was the way to do the business when you're blagging off banks and post offices and building societies. That sort of weapon is very frightening. It also makes big bangs and that's intimidating too. We graduated to pump-action shotguns in time. I can smell the Young's '303' gun oil, the fragrance of threat and adrenalin in it, even now. Smooth, lovely tools, are pumpers. But you have to look after them. You don't want any misfires if a team of cozzers are facing you down. Or anyone else. I always knew that my guns were reliable as myself – willing to do the business, go all the way, if required.

Handguns you must be particular about. The .38 is a very reliable gun. It's got a special catch on it which lets it off. Then you have the other ones where you can put it on a single shot. The most reliable guns I used were barrel based. And I would stick to them when there was very serious work about. I would prepare before jobs, learn everything about the weapons, be able to take them apart in seconds, keep them spotless. You fire them at walls, putting your targets up in basements, disused buildings and quiet, out-the-way areas that suddenly get very noisy from the gunshot medleys. I learned to handle every gun I ever had, even knowing just how to hold it for the best effect. Let's say I'm firing at a branch in a tree: what you do when you let one go, when you actually fire, you fire just under the branch. It'll just go up a fraction of an inch and that's when it hits the target.

It's very hard to hit something. It's a lot harder than it looks in the movies or on the telly. It's like when you see the police standing there with both hands in a locked solid stance, I know they really do get a more accurate aim. But it doesn't happen like that in gunfights in the streets or when you are being chased by armed cozzers. It's harder to hit them for they're usually hiding somewhere. They don't want any trouble these cozzers. They'd rather be giving out parking tickets. I just wanted to take the money without too much aggro or fuss. We never came to a compromise.

In the Seventies you would pay £100 or maybe £500 for a shotgun, depending on the quality. Today they are shelling out £1800 for a handgun. It's very expensive. Two grand for the very good ones, weapons like .45s. Automatic weapons, certain machine guns, are about £3,000. The other difference is the daft bastards are using them. When I was in the nick they did a survey of armed robbers and about 88 of us were questioned. They also studied armed robberies and – surprise, surprise – guns were fired in only four per cent of them. You had to be willing to hurt people but if you did it right there was no need to.

Typically, the Home Office spent a fortune on the survey. I could have told them the rules for nothing. It didn't help the cozzers or society. Today, it's the Wild West out on the streets. In London, which I know best, you're taking a chance every time you walk down the street. Some young black man with a chip on his shoulder or some young white man, and they get hold of these guns and they walk about all the time itching to use them. They want to use them, to hurt people. And all of a sudden one of them shoots a geezer and kills him.

The kid gets put in prison for a life sentence and the kid don't even know anything. It's like, 'I'm going to be a gangster.' Basically I'm so glad that the normal geezer can't get guns. The new gun laws brought in after these kids getting massacred at school in Dunblane in Scotland has worked. Only farmers or other checked-out licence holders can have shotguns ... they're in cupboards, locked up and chained up. The only gun you can have is a .22, which is not really capable of killing someone, unless it's a head shot and the bullet rattles around the geezer's brain. You've got to be really connected to get a nice gun. I'm glad because it's stopped all the cowboys getting them. There's a lot of people killing people in armed robberies and that's giving armed robbers a bad name. They're fucking idiots, they're going into cash 'n' carrys, nicking something worthless before shooting someone dead. Crazy bastards – in 2003 they nick sweets using 9mm Glocks.

There's a lot going on in the streets today that the police don't want people to know – they don't want the punters running too scared. Did you read in the papers in 2001 about the Chinese-made AR-15 assault rifle that the cozzers found in a raid? It's the sort of thing Rambo waved about in Afghanistan or Big Arnie splattered people with in *The Terminator*. Fucking horrific piece of killing machine. It can fire 950 rounds of armour-piercing bullets – they've got a titanium core – every minute. Using laser sights, and in skilled hands, it can kill from more than 400 yards.

The AR-15 was owned by a 17-year-old lad. It was discovered in his house in east London.

That's where I was born and got my first gun. It wasn't some Asian assault rifle but, as the world knows, things ain't what they used to be in the East End.

CHAPTER TWO

EASTENDERS

'JUSTICE IS ONE THING AND I AM A
FAIR MAN BUT I HAVE NEVER ASKED
FOR MERCY AND I DON'T GIVE IT.'

VICTOR DARK, 2003

I'm a true Eastender and like most of us I loved my parents. But I never wanted to be them. I always wanted more. I've always said that if I had been born with money I wouldn't have been stealing it from banks and armoured cars. But we were on the poverty line: spam, baked beans and mashed potato was a gourmet meal. I used to think I was dining posh if it was served up. If we got a fried egg on the plate as well then I felt I was in heaven, or at least the Ritz. I was a tough little kid from the start, partly because of my own hang-ups about my family's lifestyle. My mum and dad were grafters but it was a lot of effort for small reward; they saved a few shillings a week in the post office. It never made them bitter and they were always loyal to me and my brother, Tony.

I was born in Forest Gate, Stratford, on 12 April 1957. My brother is four years younger than me and basically he's a strong kid to this day is Tony. He's done very well for himself, running his own business and driving around in a Bentley.

Mum, being an east London girl, lived out in East Ham at the time she met my father one Saturday afternoon at an ice rink. It was ice-capades from the start. My father was from Malta. His father had married an English girl and in time so did his son. My dad moved to London in 1955 and had found a job at Ford's Car Company in Dagenham in Essex. So the two of them went to the same sort of spots in the area on weekends. I'm named after my dad and my mother's Lillian but I can't think I've heard anyone call her anything but Lil. They clicked when they were both young – my mum was only 18 when she had me.

Instantly, my father had a family to support. Up at six in the morning to six at night. Dagenham. I was really unaware of how tough it was until I was nine or ten years old. I thought the way we lived was how everybody lived. You grafted for every little bit you had. We existed in run-down council houses and one of the longest spells was in Ramsey Road in Forest Gate. We had the downstairs bit of the house and there was another family upstairs. They were older than mum and dad so there was a bit of friction.

Then, when I was about nine years old, we moved to Cann Hall Road in Leytonstone where, apart from prison,

I spent most of my life. It was right behind a shop, and it was one of these shops that would sell anything: a junk shop type of place. Now, it sounds stupid, but I suppose that started me off on my life of crime. I had a hang-up living behind a junk shop flogging second-hand clothes and other hand-me-down stuff. There was a side door from the shop and we lived in the back. We had to go down the side of the shop. I didn't like it being a junk shop. I had a serious chip on my shoulder when I was a kid. My dad was Maltese and we lived behind a junk shop. My mum worked in the greengrocer's next door.

When I walked around Leytonstone and Leyton, and especially in Wanstead – lots of the older kids used to use The George pub there – and looked at other kids going into nice houses with front gardens and gates and that, I was little bit, not ashamed or nothing, but I was wondering why I wasn't the same as everybody else. When I look back now I realise that a lot of it was subconscious. I didn't get teased but it was more embarrassing because if I had a girlfriend I didn't want to take her back behind the junk shop. My dad working for Ford's all the time and my mum working in a greengrocer's. We were just a breadline family really. Both Mum and Dad out at work. No telly for a long time and then only black and white and the Tardis to get us out of there with *Dr Who*.

It really reflects on the soul. When you are 12 and in your early teens, then you start to become aware of 'the haves' and 'have nots'. If mum got me a pair of trousers or a pair of shoes I'd really appreciate it and look after them. Yet it was always school stuff. If I wanted a nice pair of trousers I'd walk past the smart shops and think: 'I really want them trousers, I wonder if they'd fit me.' Things start going into your head: 'Maybe they will fit me. How could I get them?'

What started it I suppose was this geezer called Paul. I'll never forget this kid. He was a fat boy, a well-off kid. His dad had a corner shop so when we were at school together what he used to do was nick a few quid from his father. And he'd give to us. We weren't extorting it out of him – he just gave it to us. I liked having the money – and spending it on what I wanted. I really got a taste for money. So, schoolboy pranks led to thieving and on and on. It's like the idiots who get hooked on drugs – they want something harder and harder. With me, I just got harder and harder.

I'd left Cann Hall Road Primary School and moved on to the senior school before going to Leyton County High. I became mates with this George who was a Jack-the-Lad at school and much later a proper tearaway who put me right in it. As schoolboys, we were very good friends. We became a nuisance as a team, like little boys do. George was like that William Brown in the 'Just William' books: very naughty. Well, much worse than that. A real little terror. We'd try to make the other kids laugh and things like that. I'd go and buy stink bombs, which used to be in little glass tubes. George would put a stink bomb on a teacher's seat. You would hear this crunch and then this horrible smell would have us all holding our noses. George used to nail this particular teacher every time. It was just like a laugh. Finally, we got caught and we got the slipper. We used to get called up in front of the class and be given a whacking great six-of-the-best. I didn't mind taking the punishment. We'd had our fun and now we were paying for it. There's no use complaining.

I became a robber after that. Of the school tuck shop. We used to nick all the crisps and sweets and drinks. There was a big department store, Bearman's, near our place and lots of the kids had great toys but Mum and Dad could not give me these things. Other kids would ask me: 'Do you like my Scalextrix?' I would go to me dad and ask for a Scalextrix and my dad used to say, 'No, we haven't got the money for that.' We didn't have the money so I started stealing the stuff, petty thieving it was.

As I got into it, I got more brave. I became a cocky little bastard. At that age you think you can do the business, no matter what the odds. What a chancer I was. I started with little things and then it got bigger. It became easier. I had got more organised by the time I was 14. What my parents couldn't physically give me and I wanted I would take. I never broke into anyone's house, though. I was never a burglar. If I did creep into something it would be like a big sports shop not someone's house. I've never done that. I believed that because my mum and dad were having it hard any money I took would leave other people in rags. As I looked at it, as I got older, the big supermarkets and department stores had lots of money and wouldn't miss something.

Even at the age of 12, I was setting myself some rules. I look at what goes on today with thousands of little kids being beaten in the street for mobile phones. It makes me sick. There weren't crazes in my teenage days for phones and trainers or Ralph Lauren jackets. Stuff people are willing to kill for today. I wasn't trying to compete with people. I just wanted the stuff, so I took it – but from the big boys, not from other kids in the street. Straight away, I knew what to do and what not to do.

I wanted to join a youth club called The Pastures in Leytonstone but I was still too young. I wanted to get there because I was interested in girls and that's where they went. But I wasn't, at 12, that sexually advanced. I was still into frogs and newts! The thing about The Pastures was that it had a massive pond at the back which was swimming with frogs and newts. Me and my cousin used to sneak around there to catch them. But there was a caretaker called Steve and if he caught anyone he used to enjoy flogging them with a cane. We wanted our fun but not the pain. I used to hide in the bush and keep guard for my cousin Harry.

Harry and I were at it for about a month and the geezer was on to it that two little rascals were creeping over and nicking his newts. One night, I can't believe it: I'm standing there and my cousin is leaning over the pond and I see the caretaker with his cane, towering behind him. Steve had been waiting for us. I had no choice – I ran out, full pace, and straight into this big Steve bastard and pushed him. He went face first into the pond. I was only a kid and he was a grown man so if he'd caught us he would have killed us. But he didn't catch us. He was still rubbing the water from his eyes as we were out of there like bullets. That was the first test of loyalty to a mate – you do anything to get a friend out of trouble. It's just, in later life, that the odds and the consequences get far more serious: life or death serious.

When I was 14, I joined The Pastures and Steve was still working there. He used to give me glances but I don't think he ever really knew if I was the one who ponded him. But he eyed me.

At the club there was a gang of older boys who used to shove me and my friends around. I was just a middle-sized child and I had long, fair hair then. I used to have big ear lobes (I'll tell you about my personal plastic surgery with a pair of nail clippers later) and covered them with my hair. Maybe they thought I was up for a beating for they were a lot of skinheads – jeans rolled up, braces, crombies and big stalk boots. I must have looked a right little Fauntleroy to them: someone just right for a kicking. I was at that age when you turn from a child to a man and it's a dangerous time. You are aware of who you are and what you're about.

It's a time when lots of people take on more than they should. I wasn't ready to go against great odds – yet. But, as it turned out, I didn't have to. I wasn't going to take anything from them but they picked on my mate Johnnie first and gave him a right good slapping. It wasn't directly personal to me so I felt I could 'phone a friend', as it were.

I resolved not to take them on alone. I went to the pub my dad used and he rounded up my cousins who were mostly 16 and 17 years old. We made a plan and I swaggered back into The Pastures as though I was on the Yellow Brick Road. The bovver boys went apeshit. This skinhead bunch came raving after me but I took off out of the club and up the street. They ran right into my cousins who got hold of the bastards and blinded the bleedin' daylights out of them. Feet, fists and the head – on all of them a few times. I managed to get a few in myself – but, hey, I was only little. They shouldn't have picked on me.

That was the start, for me, of tit for tat, violence for violence, an eye for an eye. I knew where to draw the line but if I thought I was going to get done over I would take the other lot out first. It was a lesson in tactics. And in the universal law and respect of aggression. But, mostly, a graduating course in the power, the influence, of violence.

Guess which gang I was asked to join next? So, there's me with my long, blond hair and this bunch of skinheads. All mates together. We were all too young to go in pubs and that, so it was local discos and hanging out in the streets. I was in my mid-teens and had been chased and bumped about a few times when I had a fight with this geezer but as I'm fighting him fair and square another bloke comes up and hits me on the head with a bottle. I thought I should have known that was coming – I joined a karate club. Thirty years later I still do karate. It has saved my life many times through the discipline, self-control, physical endurance and the attack and defence skills it teaches.

Of course, by then I didn't just want to look after myself but also the ladies. At that age, like most kids, I was a walking hormone waiting to explode.

I wanted to show off to the girls, to impress them with my smart look. My mum couldn't provide the money for that so I had to get it myself. I started to 'do' all the jewellers I could in the East End. I worked out a simple plan: in those days they had a silver stripe across the window which was all that was protecting all the watches and gems on display. I got myself a catapult and a supply of ball bearings. A ball bearing or a marble travelling at a certain speed will make a hole – it will not smash the glass because it's so fast. A few cracks but little noise. Do it at night with one mate watching – you didn't need a gang and it kept the expenses down – and it was a little bit of fun. And profit.

Nine out of ten you would get jewellery out of that hole, which was about an inch wide, with a bit of wire bent into a hook. Any time I felt like a bit of fun I'd reach for the catapult and it would be a late fry-up at Tiffany's. But mostly I did H. Samuel down any other High Street.

I really started getting right into it then. I would sell the stuff on to local people. That's where I got the money to buy fancy clothes to impress the girls. The jewellers to me were like wealthy people who weren't going to miss a few rings and chains and things like that. They'd just be pissed off that they'd been done.

I had a lot of buyers and sellers at an early age. I was brought up in that sort of world. It was petty money. With my mates we moved on to robbing trains, usually at the main railway stations. We weren't hurting no one. We would creep into the freight yards, take the security locks off – a good pair of pliers would do it – and take whatever looked tasty out the back. You'd get parcels and consignments of things like leather coats, which you could always move on. The good thing was you could walk into a pub around the East End and say, 'Look, this fell off the back of a lorry,' and make loads of sales. Not a word was said. It was living in the world of Oliver Twist except there was no Fagin and I was being artful.

But, as I said, you move on. You want more. And for that you must get harder. And harder.

I was 15 years old when I got truly nasty. I know it sounds young but it depends where you're looking at it from. Today you can get by begging off the Government. I was never going to ask anyone for anything. Especially more. I wanted more but I was going to get it myself. And I was spiteful. I got into the gang thing and it's like an army. In the army you've got to be a corporal, sergeant, the general. You move up. Stomping over people as you go.

I was still at school when I got my commission.

It was a black geezer, as it happens. I was walking down to Leytonstone tube station when this black geezer bangs and smashes into me. He was half charged up a bit and he had a mate with him. I carried on walking and I looked back and I knew in my mind that these two black geezers wanted a fight. I just knew. One came up to me and he couldn't even talk proper English. I couldn't understand him. I had a long-stemmed bottle and he started coming up to me and I picked the bottle up, put it behind my back, and as he walked up to me, effing and blinding, I just smashed him with the bottle. It was like an elephant gun had hit him – it took the cocky, big grin off the front of his face with the impact. I hit him hard and jabbed at him with the bottle. His face was a mess of blood and he was trying to find his eyes with his hands. His friend jumped back, looked at me and I stared him down, challenging him to have a go at me. By then I had thrown the bottle on the street. I would have taken the other guy with my hands and he knew it. He ran off, leaving his mate swimming in blood in the gutter. Fucking tosser.

I think the respect for Victor John Dark began then.

Certainly, in the school playground. I never had a lot of trouble there.

But it was then that I realised that I must arm myself properly. Broken bottles were for punters in pub fights. I needed the real tools like big Stanley knives that could take an arm off if they had to. A gun would be nice too. A great big fucking gun. As it turned out, for the more immediate enterprises, hammers were to be more useful. At the football. And the banks. I found out early that you had to find the specialised tool for the trade you were in. And if you fuck up, don't blame the tool ...

CHAPTER THREE

THE HAMMERS

'THE AMOUNT OF BOTTLES THROWN
AT MY PLAYERS WAS SCANDALOUS.'

**DAVID O'LEARY, FORMER MANAGER OF
LEEDS FOOTBALL CLUB, FOLLOWING VIOLENCE
AT HIS TEAM'S FA CUP MATCH WITH CARDIFF
ON 6 JANUARY 2002**

I had to laugh, just after the New Year and World Cup 2002, happening to read the headlines all about 'FA Cup Mayhem' and brutality and violence on the terraces and on the pitch. What was different about Britain? We had rail strikes and the rain and damp – and football violence. Déjà fucking vu? You bet. It was as if I had never been away. I watched the fighting after the Leeds and Cardiff City game on the telly and it looked like some foreign country with the cozzers all decked out in riot gear and the batons held above their heads, ready for action.

But what had made me smile was that they were complaining about liquor bottles being chucked at the players and the poor old ref. In my day with the West Ham supporters we supported the Hammers – with hammers.

Not bottles. Hammers. Of everything I have done what upsets me most is the soccer violence. It was not a man's place to be. It was stupid and it was pointless. My only explanation was that I was a teenager and, at that time, had not learned better. The moment I realised how pointless and pathetic it was, I walked away. People were being maimed and killed for no reason, certainly not for profit. It was moronic. When you get older, you think it would settle down. It never will – just look at what happened at Ninian Park in January 2002. Soccer violence is not for grown-ups.

And I wasn't a grown-up when I was in the middle of it. There was a real social upheaval going on when I was a teenager in the Seventies; I never got the same rush from it as many others did. It was like the movie *Saturday Night Fever* where John Travolta works in a dead-end job in a paint shop all week and then on weekends becomes a disco king in a white suit. At the football, all us John Travoltas got the adrenalin going, and got off on seriously kicking the shit out of rival fans. Football violence was part of Britain when I was growing up, part of my life, but I don't think looking back it could have been much different. I just think kids in 2003 are going the same way – when opportunity looks like a brick wall you soon start to kick at it with all you've got. Something nasty always happens when you hit a barrier. Somebody always gets splattered.

In the early days of the Seventies when we had strikes and strife and Harold Wilson or Ted Heath talking bollocks, the distraction for the politicians was football violence. They kept talking in Parliament about the evil disease of soccer violence and shouting about it in the papers but they did nothing because there was money to be made. Being Saturday afternoon gladiators kept the mobs happy. I think some of the commentators, Brian Moore and the rest of them, got more mileage barking on about the off-pitch violence than any of the stuff on the field. Football violence wasn't, and still isn't, anything to do with sport or team. Who gives a fuck who's winning when some bastard's got a big knife at your throat and you're trying to stab him in the bollocks? The telly results man saying, 'Manchester United, one, West Ham, two' is of no interest. All you are interested in is staying alive and taking home the other bloke's bollocks as a trophy. The FA Cup? In those days the chant for that was 'You're Gonna Get a Fucking Kicking …' It wasn't cricket but, then, we were using cricket bats or snooker cues to knock the shit out of the other lot. Rules? Staying alive was the only rule.

The beautiful game? What tiresome bollocks. Let me give you some of the truth of it. We were all happy to be tough, young lads and didn't want to be talked down to by politicians or anyone else. For my teenage generation of West Ham 'supporters' we became the violence kings of the terraces – Upton Park was our home turf and gawd help anyone who tried to take liberties there. Of course, they all did, especially the Manchester United lot. The thing about the soccer bangabouts was that anyone could join in. You just had to have the nerve to join the mob and go for it.

I soon learned who had the bottle and who didn't. I had already realised I needed to be organised with a good, strong gang and with weapons. I had got tools on board like knives and other stuff – but no guns, yet – and from then on was expecting no mercy – or to give any. If we'd graduated to guns on the terraces I can't imagine what might have happened to all of us, to the country really. We'd have been a Banana Republic 30 years earlier.

Most of the teenage gangs got their rocks off on Saturday with the football. The rest of the week we were just trying to kill ourselves. This was a positive distraction in my mind – at least we were going to kick the shit out of people we didn't know. Teenage gangs. A lot of them were into football at the time and quite often my mates were Arsenal supporters. I'd always been, like my father, a West Ham fan. But, as I said, the rumbles were nothing to do with football. I don't think half of these geezers could name the team. With the little gang I was in, I quickly found out who would stay and fight and who would run. And who was a coward. I would learn more about all of them as time went on. They were just a bunch of strong, wiry kids like me who wanted something. We were singled-minded people who would not be appeased by comic books or daft telly. Reaching out for something and kicking shit out of people on a Saturday was the result. It was not a good result but it was the reality of it. The same as it is today. New Labour? Same old shit. This time they are going nowhere but making it take longer. Distractions? Everyone needs them.

The violence was escalating every week and it was getting really nitty gritty. We started to become a little firm to be reckoned with. We fought as a team and looked after ourselves that way as well. In my early days the Chad Heath (Chadwell Heath) gang was the one to be in, and that was the forerunner of the InterCity Firm (the ICF) which is still infamous. The ICF became notorious for not giving a shit what they did or who they hurt. When I was robbing banks they were still kicking the shit out of each other. Silly fuckers.

The ICF got its name because of kids who were broke and could not go to away matches by car or in lorries. Many went on the trains and most of the fares were fiddled or on the cheap. I never paid for a train trip – I just walked on. When I had to. I liked going in vans with the lads – it was a lot easier to get away from the trouble. But for lots of them an awayday ticket was a passport to rioting and really fucking up as much of the country as possible. I now wonder why any straight fucker ever took a train on a Saturday. Or even went out of the house. I often used to puzzle about it and I was in there with the boots and fists just like all the others.

Our speciality was the hammers. Short, stubby pieces of

wood with awesome great weights on the end of them. Stick that in someone's face and they'd take a week to come out of casualty. Bang them on the head with it and they'd need Dracula and his firm to get them back from the dead. Soared through the air at a football match and the hammers just knocked the fuck out of whoever they hit. Well, I suppose that's what we thought. If we thought at all in those days of, when I look back on it, chilling violence. No one gave a fuck. It's like that song 'It's Raining Men' by Geri Halliwell. In my football violence days it was raining horrible hammers. If a hammer had killed the Queen a chant and cheer would have gone up. Skinhead, working-class violence ruled. Fuck the rest of you. I was involved but I never truly bought it. I couldn't see the profit.

I have always been willing to be a bad bastard but always for profit, for a return.

I never had that drop of evil madness which seemed to have baptised so many of the people around me on the terraces. Mob violence is the most terrible thing to witness, like a river that's burst its banks – it's going where it wants to go and there's no stopping it.

Not that I want off the hook. I threw the hammers. Better and harder than most of them. And we hit targets. We were the Musketeers of Saturday afternoons. And we had the whole East End with us. I was always concerned about the soccer violence. I just did it because everyone else did. I now know how senseless it was. But, at that time, I was trying to prove myself, show what a gladiator I was. I understood later that I did not have to prove myself to anyone.

When you do an armed robbery – despite that description of it – there's very rarely anyone hurt. But in the football when I was a kid, people were getting hurt. I never could understand why a 16-year-old was going to stab someone just because they supported another fucking football team. A lot of people were getting killed at that time. And a lot of it was covered up by the football authorities and the police. It was bad PR.

It was our little firm on the terraces, about ten of us that followed me into the banks and the rest. They are still names in my former business a quarter of a century later and let's just call them Col and Ralph, the two Rays, Richard, Matthew and Terry. Disciples in the gospel according to Vic. I'm an SAS believer – Who Dares Wins!

We always won. What I learned most of all from the football violence was how to take on a crowd and that paid off later when I robbed banks and building societies packed with customers trying to do their business. When you have been one of ten against five hundred seriously nasty people keeping a bank queue in line is babysitting. Your nerve isn't jumping, which is the secret. It is all about control – and self-education. I was an early learner. I have always had a quiet nerve.

I was a youngster when I started going to the football; I liked to watch the bigger boys take the piss. Some of the old Mile End lot were proper men, really big guys and tough. I was just a kid and they impressed the hell of me. One was called Baptist and there was lots of fire and brimstone from him and the rest of them. The first real taste of it I got was when we went up to Sheffield United.

We'd just got to the ground and all of a sudden a big crowd was running towards me, about 40 geezers: it was like all of *Coronation Street* was running at you, a great big bunch of northerners. My mind told me to run but it also told me that if I did I would be leaving my mates behind. I stood my ground. I was an Eastender. There was a massive punch-up. I had never seen casual violence like it. People's faces said they would kill you just for the pleasure of it. No reason, simple delight in the violence of it all, the blood and the broken bones that I saw sticking out of arms and legs. I saw all these faces smashed in with bricks. There were other tearaways with big planks of wood and using them like hammers and swords, banging and stabbing and hurting whenever they hit a target There were no guns or anything like that. This wasn't a firm, just men you knew who could do the business. It was a good early lesson to be prepared for anything. The rest, the Mile End mob and the ICF, followed all too easily.

I was doing a little work elsewhere – pretty profitable armed robberies, as it happened in my later teens – so, being a bandit, I was the one who introduced the masks at football matches. Masked football hooligans became a big thing.

It made sense to me that if you were going to be on camera in the thick of it the last thing you wanted was your mug on film. It was also more intimidating to the other lot. There were lots of them that thought they were Batman or the Lone Ranger but all they were were just silly fucks wearing masks. I used to wear a Richard Nixon mask like the robbers in America did. Half of them never knew he'd been President of the United States. Me, I just didn't want the telly cameras to know who was kicking the shit out of who. It was out of order but the masks still make sense to me. You can still see the crowds wearing masks on the terraces in 2003.

We had a hard core at every match of between ten and 15 lads. You didn't sign up to the firm. You became part of it – only after you proved yourself. The East End was West Ham, so obviously if we wanted a fight with west London, it would be Chelsea. If it was north London, it would be Tottenham. It was all different firms or factions but all singled-minded about having a riot.

The biggest one I was involved in was against Chelsea who had just gone down to the Second Division. That didn't help the hooliganism, as all the fans were pissed off. I was 17, and West Ham were to play Chelsea and about 30 of us met up at the Swan pub in Stratford in east London. All my close friends were with me: tough bastards, and the unofficial leaders of the ICF. It was a London Derby, the East End versus the West End. We were all up for it. Even in the pub, people knew it: they kept looking at us and there was that atmosphere of impending catastrophe. For one lot or the other.

We went into the Chelsea Potter pub in the King's Road and there was this big blonde bird and a little fella. It was the wrestler Mick McManus who was there having a quiet drink but he didn't hang around when we got there. He could sense that atmosphere – some tough guy.

Then we went walkabout. The police were all over the place, with West Ham versus Chelsea they were expecting a major kick-off and I don't mean the one starting the game at 3pm. None of us wore or carried supporters' scarves. We didn't want to be identified. Yet I thought they were going to discover we were West Ham so I got our firm singing, 'We're the North Stand, We're the North Stand', trying to make them think we're the Chelsea mob.

When we got to Stamford Bridge there were some of West Ham, our lot, already in place, part of the Wooden Horse plan. They had 'The Shed' then and there were these stairs, a neck of stairs which took you right into the North Stand – the Chelsea end. But that daft Chelsea mob had no idea who we were. They're looking at us chanting 'The North Stand' and they are wondering who are these geezers. A right lot of nasty bastards was the answer.

At the same time the cozzers were all but throwing us into the Chelsea end as they tried to keep the crowds moving. The police were saying, 'Get in there, get in there' and throwing us in the Chelsea end. We walked up the stairs and by the time we got to the top we were a lot taller. We were saying to each other, 'Hold the line', like that Russell Crowe did in *Gladiator*.

It was a full-capacity crowd and we were spreading out to make more impact when we identified ourselves to the other lot. It was 20 minutes before the official kick-off; just the right time for ours. I saw the other West Ham mob that were in there and shouted: 'United!' A full battle started which went on for about 15 minutes. It was fierce and lots of people got seriously badly hurt. Every person seemed to be bloodied somewhere on their body. We had steamed right into them. It was just hands and fists. Eventually, we all ran on the pitch – got right in the middle of it, still punching and kicking the fuck out of each other. The West Ham fans at the other end were chanting, 'We're proud of you', and screaming support for us.

The Old Bill had a serious problem. They couldn't put us back in the North End together or the battle would have just gone on. And then bricks started coming in at us and people are getting seriously hurt. It was at that moment that, for the first time in my life, I was pleased to see a cozzer. He came up to me and started saying, 'If I see you fighting ...' but he was rudely interrupted when a brick hit him on the back of the head. If he hadn't been there it would have hit me straight in the face. He went down in a dead fall. I found out later that this was all over the telly.

The police were behind us now and trying to push us back into the stands. I tried to break the goal crossbar for a giggle, just a bit of rebellion as they were shoving us about, and then the fun was over – the game started.

The ICF were a special organised unit then and we started doing our awaydays, especially up north where we were always heavily outnumbered. We used to be crazy. We were gangs of geezers. There would be 50 or 60 of us in vans but the rest built up their armies on the trains. The ICF used to travel all round the country on the trains and that's how they got their name, InterCity Firm. I got enough trouble on the roads so I only took the train when I had to. They, of course, were never on time, which just made us all feel angrier. InterCity rail had much soccer violence to answer for.

On one trip to Liverpool there was a massive fight all the way. We bumped into some Wolverhampton supporters and I knocked one out with a snooker cue. That's before we even got to Liverpool! When we got to Liverpool we couldn't get into the ground – it was full and closed to any more 'fans' who wanted to see Liverpool play. We're locked outside and we're frustrated by this. The Old Bill marches us round to Everton's ground. Everton's playing away and suddenly all the Everton reserve players come running out to play some other northern mob. Their faces were a picture when there was this almighty 'United' and they realised an army of West Ham supporters were there.

They were dumbstruck, wondering where we'd all come from. We waited our time and about half an hour before the end we got out of the ground and made our way up to the Scouse end. We got in and when they opened the gates we had a massive big punch-up there. It was running battles all day.

Like everything else, good or bad, reputations depend on where you are standing, and viewing them from. In the early Seventies the Manchester United fans had a terrible name – they were good at mob violence. Football violence was really becoming an art form then and United were bashing everyone up.

United, like other northern clubs, wanted to fight London's Eastenders who wanted to take on the south Londoners. The south Londoners were going to fight the north Londoners. As I said, this wasn't anything to do with football. It was about who was going to be the hardest out of the little firms at that time. It would start outside. You would get your little firm and you'd wait for them and they'd wait for you. Patience was part of the building of excitement, essential to the thrill of it.

After about two years, most of the mobs wouldn't come to Upton Park. It was so feared at the time, our little firm. Manchester United were always up for it and that was when the hammer attacks I told you about started. One week we knew the Manchester mob were coming so we went into all the ironmongers in the East End of London and bought up hammers and chisels and shotput-like iron balls. We were going to defend our castle! If we could have figured out how to have molten lead we would have gone for it. This was going to be the mother of all rows.

We were the Hammers – and this Saturday we were going to show them why. The violence was immediate. We were only about 40-handed but we held our own against their mob of more than 100, maybe more, before the game started. Then, the football began. And more fun for us. When the match settled in and the other lot are all shouting 'United' – the atmosphere just right – we all looked at each other and myself and the other throwers flung out the hammers. One at a time, like cannon shot. The manner might have been medieval but the effect was electric.

There's a chant of 'United' and a hammer goes and moments later some poor bastard is stretched out. There's another 'United' and another hammer soars in the air and another poor bastard hits the ground. With an almighty, awful thump. That day they were stretchering them off every few minutes. Of course, the riots started and we were fighting all day. Hammers and chisels into the opposition. It hammered home West Ham's dominance off the pitch. We were the firm to fear. There were more than 120 people seriously hurt that day. Football violence had begun in a terribly turbulent way in the mid-Seventies.

It got worse. People were getting stabbed. It was getting dangerous for all of us, no matter how good we were. I was carrying knives. I stabbed a lot of people. I was getting fucking nasty. When I thought I might have killed a man – for no reason whatsoever – I stopped. I walked away from the terraces and that senseless violence. Someone had nearly died and that was it for me. I didn't see the point. I grew up at that time. I'm not saying I stopped being violent, I'm saying I stopped being young and silly. What was the point of it all? Those rumbles were far more serious than anyone ever let on. If we went to some of these bigger grounds like Newcastle there were thousands of bad boys wanting to rip your head off. I've taken on a police horse – it won, knocking me arse over tit. I've seen my mates flung into front gardens in some of the mayhem. Loads of people got cut and slashed and they did the same as us. One guy, Paul Dorset, got stabbed through the heart by a load of Millwall supporters and nearly died. I had stabbed people and realised how close it had come to death.

It was gang warfare. It wasn't football. It was an excuse. I didn't go for the football and neither did they. It was like a pecking order and who could be the hardest. Who'd have the most bottle.

There were a lot of terrible prices being paid for excitement. Once on a trip to Liverpool the city's streets were just full of fucking hooligans. I had a hard core of people who wrapped around me, who would die for me. I didn't want them to die for no reason. I just stopped doing it because someone nearly got killed. And I thought that was enough for me. I tried to persuade my mates to do the same but with little success. At 17, I was sick of football violence.

Earlier, I had found a great escape from it with karate. I had joined a class in Forest Gate with an instructor called Peter Spanton who had been a European Champion. I worked with him for four and a half years and got my brown belt in karate. He was a tremendous influence. He and karate instilled discipline in me and knocked the bully out of me. It was a nice thing. When I walked into a karate class after being seen as a soccer hooligan – someone that didn't give a fuck for anyone – I entered a new world of thought and discipline with karate.

When you went into the karate class you had to bow, out of respect to the hall. If you didn't you had to go back out again and walk back through that door and bow. The real meaning of respect was driven home to me by the discipline of karate and by Peter Spanton. In all my time with him I competed in many competitions all over England. I also got involved with judo for two years and I spent 18 months learning kick-boxing, always working with the very best available to me. It was violence but controlled, orchestrated and with a purpose. I learned how to use my mind as well as my physical abilities.

Football violence had given me the edge on doing things in crowds of people. Control. I learned that if you had five staunch people against 40 people who didn't have all their heart and balls in it, you could stand your ground.

Karate gave me discipline and resolve. The gypsy fellow sold me the .410 shotgun. I had the parka coat so all I had to do was sling the gun under it so it was easy to swing into action and to bring terror. By the time I turned my back on football I had a full-time job as an armed robber. For the first one, an East End building society, there was just myself and a friend who had some bottle. I said to him, 'Do you fancy it?' He did. My career as an armed robber officially began that day when we blagged about four grand in four minutes.

For a teenager, even after the split, that seemed like a good rate of pay. All I wanted was bigger guns and amounts of money. It arrived – fast.

CHAPTER FOUR

VIOLENT TIMES

'WE WERE THE AGE OF BOY SCOUTS
BUT WE WERE ARMED ROBBERS.'

**VICTOR DARK RECALLING, IN 2003,
THE START OF HIS TEENAGE CRIME SPREE**

I was a villain, a bad boy, from an early age. And I do think it's easy to understand. You take what you can't have. I found that out quickly in the East End of London.

I'd had a few girlfriends and I wanted to impress them. I spruced myself up through petty thieving. Did I have the best new pair of jeans? You fucking betcha. And the tops and all the gear. My mother used to go apeshit wondering where it all came from. I told her my mates gave the stuff to me. It was easier for her to believe that than that I was nicking cashmere jumpers and the like. I did have taste even in those days – I went for the best.

I was also getting really fit – in the physical sense. I worked out and I ran every other day. I had lots of strength and muscle. The brick wall was not going to stop me. It was just that the only path I could imagine to becoming something was to make myself clever, highly rated, at being a very bad boy. I became so strong that at times I would impress myself. That's not boasting: I thought of that, of being truly as fit as possible, as being part of my trade. You have to work out to get the best out of life, no matter what trade you go into. If you venture into armed robbery then there is a definite advantage in being able to leap over counters and run like fuck if you have to. The cozzers trained on tea and doughnuts and, as far as I hear, still do. I was in the gym. It's all about how much you want to win and as a teenager I wanted it badly.

Almost as much as I wanted Sue – and her lifestyle. I met Sue at a disco in the East End. She was like something off a movie screen with everything prominently in all the right places. For a growing young lad she was awesome, a package you wanted to sign for. I got to know her very well and all of sudden she said to me, 'I want you to come and meet my mum and dad.' I wasn't that keen. What teenage boy wants to be checked out by the parents? She lived in Wanstead which to me was the Beverly Hills of east London. It was a real Tory stronghold and all those folk who thought they were something belonged to 'the Con' club – it was the Conservative Club but they all called it 'the Con' and maybe it was. I thought it was a huge joke. There were baker shops and butchers and it was all quaint, more like the Fifties than the Seventies: lots of little old ladies, all dressed up to do their shopping, people walking dogs on the green. Even the tube station was a listed art deco building. What a life! Her dad drove a black cab and they had quite a bit of loot. I can tell you that I did not want to upset her – no red-blooded man would – so I went around to the house. It was as stunning as Sue. The house was absolutely beautiful. It was full of grand settees; in every room there were big, sparkling chandeliers. For me, it was a bright, shiny new world.

Apart from taking the piss out of the teachers, school had nothing for me and I left as soon as I could and, at 15, I was training as a motor mechanic engineer. It was real dirty work at the garage and the geezer who ran the place was a prick. He thought he was in the RAF with his big, handlebar moustache. He worked with his son who was a bigger prick than he was. I gave them the shove and moved to another garage but the money was nothing. By the time I'd given my mum some money for living at home and had paid my bus fares, that was it. My dad kept saying, 'Don't worry, son. It'll all come when you get older – you'll earn the money.' I knew that was bollocks. I looked at my dad and what had happened in his life was really playing on my brain. He was always moaning about his health, his ears, and the more he went on the more I thought, 'Aw fucking hell.' And he had bad feet too! He wanted me to go and work at Ford's like him. My priority was how the fuck to get out of the situation. I was going nowhere. I had a job on the railways at weekends banging clips into the tracks with big hammers, a very useful experience as it turned out. That gave me some extra cash to top up working as an apprentice mechanic. But there was never enough money for what I wanted to do, for the lifestyle I wanted and saw other people living.

I wanted it so badly I can still feel it today. I was prepared to risk everything for it. And that's the point. You have to be prepared to take on the odds, take the risk and go for it. No point in talking about it in the pub. That's where strength of character matters. You want it? You have to be prepared to fucking go for it – and take the consequences if it all blows up. I wanted it more than anything. That was when I met the gypsy, a little fella called Wally – what a stompin' fucker he was – and bought my first gun. One of the boys I knew at school had just got his Boy Scout badge for orienteering. At least he knew where he was going.

The first job was a bit of a sweat but it got easier when we got into the pace of it. There was this building society in the East End – there were so many of them I can't recall the names of all the places we blagged – and I used to walk past it every other day. There were two geezers and a bird behind the counters and I knew they were handling lots and lots of cash. I thought I should have some of that. I worked it out as a two- or three-hander.

We were just kids but we knew the score. I spent three

weeks working out the times of when they went to lunch, when the money was picked up and what was the best day – Thursday. I would work out the situation and then go into a shop and say, 'Sorry, mate, I've just knocked a cat down. Where's the nearest police station so I can report it?' Worked every time. I could pinpoint where the cozzers would be coming from and how much time we had to do the work.

I did it with just one other guy. We went in like bandits: the full gear, boilersuits and masks – just like we'd seen in the movies. It was then I learned the power of the gun. I swung it from under my parka and the whole place became mine. As I said, you can curse and shout but swing that big fucking gun around at them and you have control. We had control. And we had the money.

Then, of course, I wanted more. I thought we should be knocking off the security vans with all the cash they carried. But to do a van you need to be able to drive a van. At our age we didn't have the vehicles – and we hadn't passed our driving tests! So we went on doing building societies and post offices.

I would sort out the best venues and times. I had a couple of guys to work with who I trusted. Still, I would sweat it out until the moment we burst in and started the action. Then, there was no fear. I knew I had control. I loved it, the feeling of authority and being professional about it. We were never out to hurt anybody – we were there to steal the money. That was the job, the purpose.

As in any profession, you get more ambitious. I saw opportunities that were more of a risk and I took them. I'd updated the weapons and we had a couple of 12-bore shotguns which had not been easy to buy. When you're as young as we were you don't have the contacts. At that time no one would take us seriously. I was 17 and an armed robber – 'fuck off' was the adult reaction.

But we managed to make the connections. I found that I could get guns on a sale-or-return basis. If you used them you paid for them but if they were never fired and could be sent out again I paid a 'rental' fee. I was never conscious of saying to myself 'Who can I ask?' Because we were all so young we couldn't find anyone to respect what we were up to. It was very hard to convince older people to get the guns and equipment we needed to upgrade our robbery business.

The grown men, they ain't interested 'cos they believe that as soon as you get caught you're going to grass them up. Getting to the hard core of the business took time. Yet, it was easier when I found an 18-year-old who could drive lorries. He came out of Chelmsford and was able to find people to help and other assorted benefits: guns and cars and other tools of the trade.

We became the legendary sledgehammer gang. A woman had been shot in a bank raid and they had installed these great fucking screens to protect the tellers. It was very, very hard to get through these screens. I managed. We had a sensible little firm: there were four of us. I trusted each one of them. I knew they would die for me just as I would die for them. We were the Four Musketeers.

Our testosterone was overflowing.

My railway work gave me the idea of the sledgehammer to get through the screens. I knew that if the impact was at the right point that protection would go. I just had to get the points rights: one, two, three and four – four proper smashes with the hammer, a matter of seconds, and we were in. It sounded simple but, of course, your balls are bursting at the moment of impact.

It all had to be done with precision and planning. The cars would be stolen from miles away from the target. We'd have cars waiting at different spots so we could switch as often as necessary. We certainly weren't running into the places and shouting: 'Stick 'em up – give us the money.' On the sledgehammer gang, we used to do the same sort of thing every time. We'd wear two sets of tops, say a white shirt and a black shirt, one over the other. On the robbery you'd have the light shirt on top and as soon as you came off the robbery you'd rip it off and drive away from the work.

All the witnesses remember the shirt and the cozzers are off track. You're not going to get pulled. We had a different sort of uniform from the sorting offices and, later, the banks. It was always a normal-looking but baggy coat to conceal your tools, the shotgun and the hammer. I couldn't really sleep the night before a raid – worrying if it was going to go right: were all the plans, the cars, in place? It was good to be worried, it made me check things through in my mind. It was a cross-check of all our preparations. You plan these things as best you can but there can always be mistakes if you don't keep on top of every detail.

With the sledgehammer gang I used to go and buy a hammer for every job – I always left the hammer behind. The build-up to it is the same. At that time I would wear a stocking mask with a peaked cap or just the stocking mask on its own. I pulled the mask down as I went in – it gives such an evil look. I'd go straight through the doors, get everyone to lie down, attack the screen straight away with the sledgehammer: one top corner and then the opposite bottom corner, same again, and then an almighty smash in the middle (I never had trouble with the post office and building society screens). By then I'd dropped the hammer, pulled out my shotgun and had the place covered. My mate, who was a little fella, would jump through the hole and he and another geezer would start taking the money out of the tills.

At 17, I had a big business going. But we were still learning and always after a quick earner. Up where I lived there was a fella who owned a big clothes shop. His place was always busy, so we thought he'd be good for some easy money. Like clockwork, he used to go to the bank every

Friday with this package, which we supposed was the week's takings. There was no CCTV in those days, so we planned to rob him in the street. We monitored his movements, arranged a getaway car – a Mark III Cortina – and a driver. The job was set up. The plan was no guns – I took a water pistol to stick in his back, give him a fright. But, as a precaution, I filled the water pistol with ammonia.

On the day we took him he ran a little late and it was nearly 1pm when I slipped up behind him and put the 'gun' in his back. He started shouting and struggling – he didn't care about the 'gun'. I got my arms around him but he put up a fight. There was surprise and amazement on his face but he was angry. I thought he must be carrying lots of cash, maybe it had been a good week at the shop. He was fighting for his life as far as he was concerned but finally he let go of the bag with the package of money. We didn't hang about but grabbed the takings and jumped into the Cortina. 'What an easy few quid,' I thought. We drove off, dumped the car and then we opened the bag up round at my mate's house. And there were the geezer's cheese sandwiches and his Thermos flask of tea. I had to laugh – what a battle he put up for a bit of Cheddar and a cup of tea.

Once, we jumped on this well-known fella. We hijacked his lorry and he said to me and my mate, 'Are you two new at the game?' I wondered what he was talking about until we discovered the load was worth absolutely nothing. The geezer who ordered the lorry hijack had to pay us £5,000 each anyway – and he was physically sick. It had cost him ten grand and what was on it was only worth about £500.

Things went better when I stuck to armed robberies. The other freelancing was too dodgy, results wise. I was careful, going small at first with building societies, which were as secure as piggy banks in those days. We would get vans and paint out the windows and use them for surveillance. We had walkie-talkies with a five-mile radius; no mobile phones in those days. Today bad boys don't register their mobiles but we had to use public telephone boxes to be secure. I'd sit in the back of the van watching and waiting. When you're actually plotting up on something it's all about the waiting game, and that's the hardest part, and where you tend to think, 'Come on, come on.'

We would usually do the biggest sorting offices we could get. We'd walk into them all over London as long as they were large and, as I said, Thursday was their busy day. And ours. I'd walk in and ask for ten stamps and I'd look over as the drawer opened and you would see how much there was. We worked out that there was about five, six, eight grand a drawer. You'd look and then come out ready for action with pump-action shotguns and handguns. We were organised as time went on – always putting money back into the business.

We kept the weapons in 'safe houses' like the IRA did.

We'd find someone with no record, someone 'straight', and pay them 50 or a 100 quid a month to look after us. The guns would be stashed in the house. You never wanted weapons near you if you got a tug on a piece of work. And we did a lot of work. And I learned quickly. You could get the protective windows out faster in the sorting offices because they were cheaper, and they were on plastic runners. The banks thought more about their customers' money, with much more solid metal runners, but that didn't stop me.

By then, we felt confident enough to take on the banks: Barclays, NatWest, the Midland as was. They were on your neighbourhood high street – and so were we. With great big fucking sledgehammers. We were also learning the game and getting more sophisticated, finding out what gear worked best for us. You had to inflict terror on the people in the bank and at the same time know what you were about – taking the money. That's what we were after – the money. The glory came later when the cozzers could not understand how we were getting away with it.

We did banks all over London. I would check them out for many days and then – all wearing the boilersuits, balaclavas and running shoes – we would burst in not too long after opening time. Then, everyone, the staff and the customers, were still a little hazy, start of the day, and we would give them the serious verbals of 'mother-fucker' and 'get down, mother-fucker', 'get on the floor, get on the floor' and the rest. I used to think it was like a nuclear bomb for some of them: spoiled their whole day.

I knew when the tellers rang the alarm bells – they also went off instantly when you hit the screens – and just how long we had to do it, to get behind the security doors. There was never more than a few minutes after that happened so I'd drag someone off the floor, put the shotgun to their head and tell the bank people: 'If you don't open the fucking door, I'm going to blow his head off.' That usually did the trick and it was quicker than smashing down a teller's screen. But I liked using the sledgehammer in the banks – it brought everyone in there to attention. The noise added to the fear. There were no security cameras in those days, so if you did the work efficiently you could be in and out before the cozzers turned up. We never worried about any confrontation with them. I didn't give a fuck. If the cozzers turned up, I was more than happy to take them on.

The bank screens were different from the building societies and sorting offices. When you actually hit them with the hammer, they would stick and you would pull it out. I would go bang, bang, bang and it would stick. I'd pull it out and go bang and it would stick. That's how it would come out: bash in all the edges and work in from the middle. I'd literally pull the thing out. I know it doesn't sound like an art form but when you have only seconds to carry it off there has to be expertise.

It was all in the preparation. We would 'twin' cars: let's say we were using a black Jaguar for the job. Well, we would then find an identical model and take the number plates and put them on the car we were using. We did the same with all the cars we used and it just led to confusion for the cozzers. After the job we had a driver to take us away. We knew which way the cozzers were coming from and we were out of there a different way.

I had a right proper, good little team. The problem with us was that we would go for it all the time. We were always up for it. Especially the sorting offices: you still have to plan and be prepared. Thursdays were our Happy Hour days: get in early when the money was still in the tills and there were not so many people around. But the number of people didn't really bother me. Sometimes there was quite a lot of people if it was a big sorting office. It didn't matter what the circumstances were – I knew I was going in there.

At the bigger post offices you'd get six or seven tills. And enough money to fill big bags. We'd have three geezers to fill the bags, a driver and me with the shotgun and hammer. We used to take fucking great bags of money slung over the shoulder from those bits of work.

But there was always the waiting before the job. I always found that the worst. And relying on other people outside of my little firm. The night before a raid I'd ring round and make sure everyone was up for it. They'd all agree and then some fucker would bottle out. There were other arseholes that I gave work to and, honestly, their arses would hit the floor; some just couldn't cope. You've got to be a special person to wanna jump out and actually commit an armed robbery when a bank or post office is packed with people. I've done quite a lot. A crowd never really scared me. I think the more people that are there, the more hysterical they are. I felt it gave me more control because nobody knew what was going on.

When you confront two or three or four people, you can get some brave person, some have-a-go Charlie. I found it was usually older people. I've had them throwing stuff at me: shopping and parcels, anything else they could put their hands on. A couple of blokes chucked walking sticks at me. It wouldn't have surprised me to see a zimmer frame flying through the air. But it wasn't a laugh – these were the scarier moments because I never knew how violent I would have to be to retain control. The last thing you want to do is use that gun. You deal with the have-a-go heroes with your fists and your hands. The last, last resort is blasting away with that shotgun. It was never necessary if you put the fear of all fears in them and I was always good at that.

I would march into those sorting offices and smash up the scales they weighed the letters on; made a hell of a noise. Once they crashed everyone would go, 'Wow, fuck' and that's why I loved the hammer. It saved a lot of confrontation with people, with the punters in the banks and post offices. It was like my karate cries. What I learned in karate was the intimidation of certain cries – I'd do my 'aaahhhhh' and people would shit themselves. Really shit themselves. That's how many of my robberies were committed. We didn't have to touch anyone because they'd just go, 'Oh, fuck.' The karate cry – Key i! – and actions looked a lot more violent than they were. It was a scare tactic.

I was scared too – of my mother. I was living at home and I was worried about her finding my money. I had about £40,000 in loot, which was a fair bundle for a young lad in the Seventies. I was piling up this money. So here I am, this big tough armed robber and I'm thinking, 'If my mum finds all this money she'll fucking kill me.' It was really weird that feeling. I kept thinking to myself, 'Where can I put it?' I knew that if my mum found out she'd go fucking mental.

When I think back, I was probably more worried about her than the police. We were just on a spree and we seemed to be able to get away with it every time. I had no qualms about the police. If they came, you shot their tyres out – I was never going to shoot at them.

I was armed and if you go that route you've got no option – you've got to come out fighting. If you get into those situations you've got to fight back.

The good thing in Britain was the cops didn't want that sort of action either. They don't like to catch you in action. I don't blame them. I never wanted to hurt anyone in those raids. It never made sense. There is a big myth about armed robbers. If you commit your own robbery there's very rarely anyone hurt. But on the football side of it when I was a kid, people were getting hurt. I never could understand why a teenager would stab someone just because they support another fucking football team. I just didn't want to kill cozzers, didn't need the aggro of that. Nevertheless, I was on bits of work when police turned up.

Most robberies at the sorting offices you can be in and out in three to four minutes. If you go in for four minutes or at the very latest five minutes, you've got to come out because you're on course with the police. You're going to bump into them, which I've done on a few occasions. Some turned out a bit more nasty than the others.

With banks I was just straight in and out. Straight in, crash through the screens, everyone, sometimes 40 people, down on the floor. You walk through and you make sure you don't hurt anyone. 'Just lie down there, mate!' and you've got a mask on and you just say, 'Stay like that, mate.' If it's a girl you say, 'All right, all right, calm down, calm down.'

When you got the bags of money you used to have to cut the fuckers with a Stanley knife they were so tough to get into. We did a place in Walthamstow in east London during our run. Let me tell you about that. There's a big zebra crossing there and our car pulled up and the place was packed outside Walthamstow market. I pulled the mask down and pulled out the hammer from my long coat.

My mates carried the guns and the bags but I just had the hammer. I had to do my thing with attitude so I went in screaming, 'Get down!!' I would go up to people and tell them to get on the floor and they would. They would be so shocked and stunned. Then I punched straight through with the hammer – I did three tills that day, dropped the hammer and my mate gave me the gun. I walked back to the front door while the others were gathering the money. I was on the main door now. I was watching front and back. I would never stand in the middle of the door. If I wanted to get shot then I would stand straight in the centre. I would always stand on the outside of the door so if anyone came in, I could jump back in. If you stand in the doorway, anyone can get you.

When you smash the windows and attack, the bells go off and it's the four to five minute rule. All of a sudden, all the tills are open. My mates have got long bags and take all the tills out and then I'd be looking at my watch and then say, 'We've got to go, 30 seconds to go.' After four minutes you're out. People who stay to open the safe never make it ...

We did a job like that in Dagenham but it went a little wrong. Someone at a bus stop saw us going in with the gear and rushed over, banged shut the latch and locked us in. We were so interested in doing the job we had no idea we were trapped inside. Until we tried to get out ... I turned around, looking at my watch, and told the team it was time to go. We try the door. The door's locked. I run round to this bank geezer and scream: 'Open the fucking door or you're gone.' I could tell by his reactions that that would have done it but it was taking too much time.

I got the hammer off the floor: the door had a glass window in it with a little wire in it, square wire. I smashed through it, taking the glass out of it. I picked up my mates and started to squeeze them through the window. They made it and I started to climb out – and the police cars arrived. I made it out and the cozzer car was right in front of me, still driving up at high speed. For once, I still had the hammer. I threw it at the car and I could see the two geezers in the car mouthing, 'Fucking hell, this cunt.' It was a big hammer and crashed into their bonnet and into the windscreen. They drove into other cars and I shouted to my mate: 'Come on, go!' I wouldn't leave until all the team was on board.

Then our preparation worked. We were roaring down the road taking all the gear off, changing appearance, we take a left, take a right, and we are the 'twin' getaway car, the 'innocent' one. We all split up. All the money and the guns would go in one bag and one geezer would be in charge of that. There would be helicopters and police cars everywhere but we had 'safe' cars and houses. I found you could always rely on good plans and preparation. People were the problem. We all met up later and sorted out our profits.

It seems we were in business, almost nine to five, five days a week: regular little businessmen. We'd crack on in Walthamstow, Dagenham and anywhere else we fancied. We did a bank up in Canning Town. We built up a pattern which took the interest of the Walthamstow Robbery Squad. All of a sudden, alerts were going out on the telly and there were stories in the papers about this sledgehammer gang. They were looking for this little firm, this sledgehammer gang. They were looking for us.

I started to think there might be problems when I went to this George's 'safe' house to put two double-barrel shotguns and a couple of handguns away. There was a van watching his flat but it fucked off and I went in there. Then the Old Bill came to his flat, knocked on the door and he talked to them and they fucked off. Why? My brain kept telling me there was something going on here. My lot of youth gangsters had become a huge embarrassment to the cozzers and they were after us in a big way. That's fair enough, part of the game, but being grassed up is another thing altogether. That would haunt me later on. I was also getting noticed for violence off the job.

I had got done in February 1976 for disorderly behaviour at a West Ham match but I got off that with a ten-quid fine at Stratford Magistrates Court. I also scraped away from a charge of cutting up a black fella. There had also been a charge of carrying an offensive weapon. The cozzers had seen me taking this lump of wood which was about five feet long and eight inches thick out of the back of this car. When it got to court they showed the 'weapon' did not even fit in the boot. I got acquitted for that. What the prosecution had done was get mixed up. It wasn't me who had the lump of wood, it was my mate: it was in his van but I threw it. They thought it was me but couldn't prove it. The problem was those antics had given the cozzers my name; I was on the books as someone who was up for action.

I was only 19 years old but I was a violent bastard and I had no fear. Pain, any harm to myself, was something that never troubled me and still doesn't. Back then, I had other things to think about. I had another job to do. A mate of mine asked me to cut up a body. He didn't fancy being a butcher's boy. Yet he was the one who had a body that needed to vanish. I felt obliged to help a mate out. That's always been my attitude – and resulted in many of my problems. I've been too fucking nice in my time.

CHAPTER FIVE

GLADIATOR

'WE BECAME GANGSTERS IN EVERY SENSE: THE FLASHY CARS, THE BEST SHIRTS, ONE OF THE BOYS. WHEN YOU'RE RIGHT AT IT AT AGE 20 YOU START TO THINK, "THAT'S IT, I'M THE BOLLOCKS." YOU BELIEVE IN YOUR OWN INVINCIBILITY.'

VICTOR DARK, 2003

He wasn't a big lad, the dead fella. I didn't know him or care to know anything about him. My friend had asked me to get rid of the body. I knew never to ask too many questions. I had agreed to help and I found myself at the back of a decaying house in Chadwell Heath, east London.

I didn't know then what I know now about violent death but I knew this geezer had taken some punishment before he gave up the ghost. In fact, he looked like someone who had come up against a really bad geezer a lot tougher than he was. There's a lot of hard bastards out there who will not take a lack of respect or suffer stupidity. They'll end a person's life without conscience. I've never been afraid of anything but butchering a body made me grow up very quickly. You have to put your mind somewhere else while you do the job.

The body was in the back room of the house when I got there and there was a big kitchen table in the room. It was one of those pine jobs that were trendy at the time. The body was covered with old sheets and blankets to soak up the blood. I thought it would be spurting all over the place but it wasn't. It just kind of dripped out of him. I didn't know how long he had been dead, but, to my amazement, there wasn't that much blood. I got the body on the table and looked at the geezer thinking, 'Poor fucker.' For all I knew, he may have been an evil little shit but lying there harmless he did look like a poor fucker. I suppose we all are when we're dead. And you certainly can't argue back about it.

I had brought along some tools for the job. I had a hacksaw, a pruning saw and a Stanley knife but had also been smart enough to bring an axe. It's amazing how tough the human body is. Dismembering a body is not an easy task and I was no surgeon. I'd bought a new set of clothes – I didn't want blood on my own gear – and I got on with the job. I felt hot and sweaty and, at times, physically sick but I just kept steadying my mind thinking the quicker I got on with it the quicker it would be over and I would be out of there.

I chopped the head off first. It was hard to get it right, to hit the right point at the neck. I didn't want to look into that face for too long or remember it, so I thought, 'I'll get rid of the really nasty bit first.' I had him rolled over on his stomach so I wasn't looking at his face. I didn't want to dwell on the face. After that it was a question of carving it up piece by piece. I used the axe on the kneecaps to split the legs up. As I did my work the other fella put the pieces into bin bags, mixing it in with real rubbish to be buried somewhere.

As I sawed and chopped I thought about undertakers and how much of it just becomes a job. Hopefully, we're all loved ones to somebody – there's unconditional love somewhere – but at the end it's just like geriatrics in the National Health of 2003: it's easier if people are dead. For fuck's sake, when you're a certain age and you go into hospital to have a toenail removed they ask if you want to be resuscitated if something goes wrong!

Of course, something had already gone badly wrong for my fella. I don't to this day know who he upset but he paid the price for it. My mate had pinched a smart little van which we could bundle the bin bags, which I thought of as the 'body bags', into. I don't recall how long the job took but it seemed like forever. There was a little gas burner in the kitchen and we made a couple of mugs of tea while it was going on. My mouth was dry and I needed the tea: it kept me alert.

I had brought lots of Dettol and bleach to clean up and I did that before we even thought of leaving. My mate was going to go back afterwards and torch the building as well. Any trace of bodies dead or alive would have been gone. I was never part of the disposal of the body so I don't know where that fella went but I suspect little bits of him ended up in fields and forests all over London. I never heard any more about it.

I had done a friend a favour. He sent me a nice little 'drink' for my birthday the following week. I was 20 years old.

I felt I could deal with anything – I didn't know that some of life's tougher lessons were about to mug me! That's the problem with being fearless. Also, I was walking even bigger in my boots. I had been given bail for a GBH, which resulted from a really nasty confrontation which I'll tell you about in a moment – you might want to have a sit down and a drink before you read about it. Back then I was a young man and feeling pretty full of myself and my abilities. I had age and fitness on my side and I thought I was invincible, not afraid of anything or anyone. Yet, I wasn't looking for trouble. We were blagging all over the place, some nice and tasty armed robberies. That was the earner, the nine to five job – I didn't need attention.

So I was trying to keep out of a lot of aggravation but it wasn't easy. When you went to clubs to meet birds there were always lots of dodgy geezers about who, like the football fuckers, just got off on hurting other people and having a good go at each other. One Saturday, I went to the

Room at the Top nightclub in the East End – I'd met a bird there the week before – and someone I knew from the InterCity Firm and three of his mates were there. We're having a drink together, the four of them and me and this bird who I really fancy; she was built for comfort. I saw a few other mates around as well but my eyes were mostly focused on the girl. A fight started somewhere in the room but it didn't seem like anything to trouble about. Then one bloke I knew comes over to me and says, 'We've got a fucking problem.' I say, 'What problem is this?' He says, 'There's a crowd of geezers over there and they are looking for bother.'

I explained that I was with someone – and had an altogether different rumble on my mind. I was adamant that I did not want to get involved but, as I would, assured him if things did 'go off' that, as a mate, I'd give him a hand. That was me being nice again. I went back to chatting up this girl and it was only later I found out there had been more trouble and a bit of a punch-up in the lift between my mates and these other geezers. There was obviously something going on and I could sense it. I told the bird I was going to the toilet and I went out to have a look at what was happening. There was Lennie – he died a few years later – and a guy called Paul, and another bloke turned around and said to me, 'There's them geezers, across the road.' He was right – there were five of them. And four of us.

I was still keeping my distance but walked across the road with the other lads, just to show support. They knew who I was and that helped my mates. Paul punched the geezer at the front and he went down. Lennie hit another one a right slammer and he went down too. The other three ran off and I thought that was the end of it. Back to the club and the bird and, hopefully, a very nice evening.

I started back to the club when I heard smashing sounds, glass being broken. And there was the noise of wood being cracked apart. It sounded very loud for three or four geezers. I whirled around and there's 28 of them – a coach party of big, hefty blokes with weapons in their hands. They were a coach party from Chelmsford. They were the Chelmsford Mob. They've gone down to the Room at the Top for a big night out, a stag party. And a rumble was going to be part of their fun.

There's the four of us – and all of them. They had broken bottles and lumps of wood in their hands. I had my big, silver hunting knife strapped into my back. I looked at my mates and they said: 'Come on, let's get out of here.'

As far as I was concerned, this was a matter of honour. I wasn't running away from anything. Nothing has ever stopped me standing my ground when there was trouble about. And in those days there always seemed to be trouble. I lived in a hard, dangerous environment but I had respect, I never attacked anyone gratuitously, for fun and games. But if someone came at me I would never stop fighting until I knew I had control of the situation. I was never going to take a beating and that often meant taking the other geezer out of the situation.

So, I looked around at my mates, and I said, 'You fucking started it.'

As I spoke all hell was unleashed. We were lined together as these 28 geezers gathered pace, rampaging towards us, howling and waving broken bottles and makeshift clubs in the air.

I walked forward. That stopped them. There I am. Alone. I've got an American flyer's jacket on and I pulled this great big fucking knife out of the strap on my back. They saw it in my hand and that stopped them. The first lot have all concertina'd into each other. That knife was like a red light.

It didn't stop 'em for long. That light turned green quick enough.

There was one big, fat bastard who thought he was up to it and he started running at me. He was going like the clappers, at an amazing speed for his size. I was coming down at him with the knife. It went straight through him, took his spleen out and then came out of his back. I have always felt that if that big bastard had not run so hard at me as I was plunging the knife into him he would not have lost his spleen. It popped right out.

There was howling from his mob – I'd just done their main man and he'd hit the floor. This geezer was getting off the floor and I kicked him straight in the eye. His eye spilt open. All my mates from the club were outside by then and saw what had happened and recognised me. This other mob – it was really weird – were falling over each other in their desperation to get away. I put the knife away and we all steamed in and got on with sorting them. That coach party got the pasting of their lives. It was like a battlefield with all these geezers lying sprawled about the gaff.

It wasn't long before there were cozzers all around us – and they were ready for trouble. They could see what they were up against and called in plenty of troops. In the stand-off, the situation began to calm down. Nobody was talking but then someone broke and it was grassed up that I had stabbed the geezer. I was very lucky as I could easily have killed him.

I was arrested for GBH and remanded in custody to Ashford Prison. I spent ten weeks there as a YP ('Young Prisoner'). It was my first taste of a nick and it was a bit of a shock. With YPs there tend to be a lot more bullies and more trouble – being young kids all these bad boys tend to think they are king of the roof.

I was taken to reception where they take all your details down: who you are, what you are, what you've been nicked for. They make you take your earrings out and give you a body search; I didn't like it standing there, naked, as they looked me up and down. Straight away it's degrading to any man. It was a really weird experience for me. One minute I was walking around on planet earth as happy as anything, the next minute I was banged up in a cell 23 hours a day. I was all right for a couple of weeks before making the court appearance. When I came back from court the authorities put me in a new cell. I'll never forget it.

All the cons had been complaining about this junkie, not wanting to share a cell with him. Everyone is going, 'Aw, don't go in the cell with him.' I returned from court and Bob's your uncle, whose cell am I in? Yes, the junkie's. I could not believe it. He'd been banging on the floor and the people downstairs had been abusing him. He didn't go out on exercise, he just stayed in the cell all the time. Obviously, I didn't know the reasons why. Unbeknown to me, all the kitchen workers were underneath my new cell.

This junkie had been jumping up and down on their ceiling and causing untold aggravation for them for weeks. They had never seen him – just heard him making this hell of a noise which kept them awake night after night. They were fucking livid. But the inmates knew me soon enough – I've always been a biggish lump and hard to miss. I was friendly enough to the junkie; no reason not to be, he wasn't jumping on my head. But he sure was beating on the floor and the others were threatening, 'We're gonna do you in the morning.' I thought it was nothing to do with me, let them crack on. The inmates had never seen the resident of the cell – cell number 52, I'll never forget it – so when I appeared for breakfast I was fingered. These geezers had seen me going in there and decided: 'That's him in cell 52.'

It was an interesting breakfast. In those days you were given little square, metal trays. At Ashford, the dining tables were in the middle of the hall and you ate there. There was a serving line down the left of the hall and the geezers from the cell below me were working on the hot plate. I get down to the front of the queue and all of a sudden some geezer goes to me: 'You bang that ceiling again, mate, and I'll bang on your fucking head.'

Out of loyalty and because of who I am, I couldn't grass on the junkie and say, 'It's the junkie jumping up and down on your ceiling.' I just stared them out but as I walked along the serving points each one of them said, 'See ya, junkie, I'm going to do you.' I thought, 'Aw fucking hell,' but I still couldn't turn round and grass the real junkie. As I was eating, I could feel the eyes on me and there was this half-caste geezer staring me out. It was really hostile. There were about 20 inmates giving me the large look.

When I came down in the afternoon they were ready for me – I could see by their faces what they were going to do. I sauntered down the queue and saw the big trouble was the geezer down the end of the line. There was a prison officer standing next to him. I got my baked beans and then I got my chips and the geezer who was causing most of the aggravation was handling the metal slice to pick up the corned beef.

As I got to his station, I saw the slice come up like a knife. I crashed my metal tray right into his face. What a splatter! The screw standing next to him had baked beans all over his head, corned beef and chips all down his uniform. He looked like a Christmas tree.

Just as quick, I found out about 'The Chicken' for the first time. It wasn't something on the menu. It involved six or seven screws jumping on me, arm locking me and holding me down, trussing me up like a chicken. I got frogmarched off to the block.

I had been given no choice about the aggro and that part didn't worry me – although the thought of twenty of these geezers out for my blood was not a happy one. I wasn't frightened, but I knew it was stacked against me and I was heavily outnumbered. What did concern me was that I was up for bail the next day. I thought that after that fracas I was never going to make bail for the stabbing.

But, bosh, I got bail. I couldn't believe it. It was like I had won the Pools. I was an escape artist. What a feeling! Nothing could stop me.

Certainly, not some big, fat Nigerian bus conductor. I was on bail for the stabbing and had gone back to work on the armed robberies but we took the weekends off. One Sunday night I was taking Sue – she was wearing one of those sexy pencil skirts – home from a nightclub called Tiffany's. We got on the bus and I said to this geezer, 'Two to Wanstead.' He took the money.

We go two stops and we're at the C&A department store stop and he shouts, 'All off! All off! Off the bus! All off!' He had taken the full fare to Wanstead, so I said to Sue we would stay on the bus, sitting upstairs. He came up and started shouting at me and calling me a 'dirty bastard'. I said to him, 'Look, mate, you've taken our money for Wanstead, now you're telling me to get off.' He's going, 'No, no, you get off the bus.' He was hanging over me with his ticket machine and I was sitting in the back seat, so I said to him, 'Play the fucking white man, mate, give the money back.'

That upset him. He took the pencil out of his top pocket and started stabbing me in the chest with it, banging it into me time and time again: stabbing me straight in the chest with his fucking pencil and screaming, 'Get off my bus.'

He was about 17 stone in weight. I was weighing in for karate competitions then at 11 stone, 6 pounds. The red buses then used to have little round light bulbs in them. The one above us had no casing. He was leaning over me, stabbing at me with his pencil and screaming.

I nutted him and caught him full in the face. That shut him up but I heard a 'ping' sound as his head bounced off the light bulb. He'd gone right back, like his head was a cricket ball, at full force and into the light.

It didn't stop him. He was a big, bad and mad bastard now. He was up for having a fight. He came running at me shouting, 'Come one, come on,' and I'm only a little fella compared to him. I butted him again and that stunned him but it didn't stop him. I got him in a headlock, turned it, but because he was so big, he was still flailing around. These headlocks take about a minute to slow someone down and this fucker certainly did not want to be tamed. He was a beast.

He managed to get me around the throat and he was squeezing so hard I felt my eyeballs popping out. I got him in the face with an elbow and he released me for a second and I had him round his fleshy throat. I was half-throttling him to keep him under control but then I just bashed in his face. He had a big bogey hanging out of a very smashed-up nose. There were people screaming somewhere; my head was spinning but I could hear the noise of people shouting and screaming charging through my head. I just felt happy. I had smashed the nasty bastard who had been totally unreasonable – and I was still breathing. That was a relief for he had given me quite a hammering before I settled him down.

I was thinking it was a good result but I should have been getting out of there for that's when about 20 cozzers arrive. They had me cornered on the bus. There was nothing I could do about getting away. They arrested me, took me down the nick, charged me and stuck me in a cell.

Apparently, I was a celebrity. The station sergeant, a cheerful bloke with a smile on his face, came round to look at this lad who's done the damage on the great, big heavyweight cunt. The sergeant came to the cell door and looked at me and did a double-take. His jaw dropped. He just couldn't believe that I had bashed this big black man up. It was a David and Goliath job, as far as he was concerned. That sergeant looked me up and down, shook his head and walked away muttering to himself.

I ended up at Snaresbrook Court in June 1978. I got done for ABH for breaking his nose. That's when the punishment for my crimes began to make an overwhelming rush at me. I was bound over for two years for 'offences against the person' but the reality of it was I got four months for the ABH and did three of them in Pentonville Prison. What a dump! It was an ancient institution and it smelled as if someone had left a sack of fish there a couple of centuries ago. It was a giant toilet and home to tramps and the like.

What got me when I arrived there was that I was the youngest person in the place even though I was no longer a YP – I had just turned 21 years old. It seems silly now but I was shocked – there were people in the nick as old as my dad. I couldn't believe how many old people were in prison – I was devastated. I thought that crime was committed by young people. It was a culture shock. I was walking down and I saw this big screw walking along holding an old dosser's shirt by his fingertips. And the dosser was inside the shirt.

It was that sort of place. It smelled but everything went

all right for me. I did my gym and exercises and the time went away. Prison is very hostile and intimidating. Everyone is trying to look after themselves. There are gangs in there, blacks, whites, every kind of race. If you fitted in you were all right, and if you could look after yourself you were OK. People inside don't know what crime you've committed when you first get slammed up. The news just gets about. It's not common knowledge beforehand. Or who you are. I walked out from Pentonville after three months but I wasn't a free man for long. The clock was ticking against me.

It was as though there was a jinx on me. I finished my stretch – and it was time to go on trial for the fracas outside the Room at the Top. I was sentenced to three years for the stabbing. Inside, I found out what violence could really be about. Pentonville had been a honeymoon. I was about to learn the reality of incarceration. Special services? Rehabilitation? Helping the vulnerable back into society? Social workers? The Prison Service wipes its arse with the *Guardian*. If you stepped out of line it wasn't counselling you received but a huge fucking kicking.

CHAPTER SIX

SCREW YOU

'I KNEW I WAS IN FOR A RIGHT KICKING SO I
WENT UP TO THE BIGGEST ONE I COULD AND
STARTED KICKING AND PUNCHING.'

**VICTOR DARK, 2003, ON HIS SERIOUS INTRODUCTION
TO BRITAIN'S PENAL SYSTEM**

My little armed robbery firm had been doing nicely. We were all over the place, planning our targets and pulling off some smart jobs. Yet once again I was in the dock of Snaresbrook Crown Court and all on a point of honour. The trial went on for eight days but I knew I was going to get time for it, a street full of people had seen what happened. There's always that bit of hope but that's just the mind playing games with you, winding you up.

I was prepared for anything when I was told I'd got Wandsworth Prison for the stabbing; it had a reputation as a tough joint, somewhere where they took pleasure in 'correcting' bad boys like me. I knew there was never enough staff there and you spent 23 hours a day locked up: you got a bit of a walk around in the morning and another half an hour in the afternoon. And even before I was driven through those big, dark gates I received a taste of the 'correctional facilities' provided by that horrible antique of an establishment. I was still in Snaresbrook Crown Court – just down the road from my 'Beverly Hills' dreamland, Wanstead – when the action started, a foreboding beginning to my time. I had just got the three years and, no matter how much you expect it, there's still a crazy shock of a moment when that little hope of freedom tucked at the back of your mind is crushed. It's when you know for sure you're going to be locked up. The Wandsworth screws were there to take me away, all with silly grins on their faces that pissed me off.

I leaned over to get some photographs of my girlfriend from a folder in front of my solicitor when my hand was slapped down by one of the screws. It was just an instinctive reaction and my hand snapped back and hit the screw with a great wallop, a cracking back-hander. A temple punch. He hit me and then another one was there and he had a go too. I was going down for the stabbing and here I was being nicked for assault on a screw.

They escorted me down to the cells beneath the court and one of the screws puts his face in my face and shouts: 'You wait, you think it's all over but we haven't even started with you.' They gave me lots and lots of that, all the intimidating crap, and then we were off to Wandsworth. I was chained to screws in the van – you should have seen them! All scowling and checking the chains. Big, tough guys – and they were up for handing out punishment. Very personally. They were desperate to stick me in it because I'd hit this screw at Snaresbrook. Not one of them was pondering on the rules or rehabilitation.

When I got to dirty, scruffy Wandsworth, a massive dumping ground for the incorrigibly wicked, it was about 7pm. They marched me off to reception and I was the only new inmate there. The other new cons had gone through to the cellblock. As I stood there a disembodied voice questioned: 'Dark?' The tone was menace in surround sound. When I identified myself, the voice coldly instructed: 'In there.' A screw I had sights on pointed to a little box. I thought, 'Oh, fuck!' He said, 'Get in that box!' It was a nonce's box, I was told, where they kept all the nonces. I thought, 'I ain't going in there.' He understood what I was thinking and barked at me: 'Either you get in there or we'll put you in there.' I had a quick look around and they were about ten-handed, the big bastards seemed to have emerged from the woodwork. I was put in this box which had a little door on the front.

I'd been in this box for what I reckoned had been about half an hour when the flap of the door opened up. There was a big screw standing there and he said, 'Think you're fucking hard, do you?' I thought, 'Aw, fuck, here we go.' He put the flap back up and fucked off. Another half-hour went by and another screw came up and said, 'So you think you're fucking tough, do you? GBH and all that.' He gave it large to me as he looked through the flap. I knew I was on to something.

It was 8.30pm and I could see through the crack of the door that all the cons had gone, all the other poor fucks who went inside Wandsworth that day had gone, been 'processed'. There was only me. There were no witnesses for me.

There were about ten screws standing there. I heard a key in the door and my heart was thumping … I came out of the box and there was a counter down along the side and the screws were queued up, like Jack Palance and a line-up of Hollywood bad guys. I could see what they were going to do. They told me to get to reception. I got to reception and a screw says, 'Take all your clothes off.'

I thought, 'Fuck that.' I knew I was going to get a kicking anyway, so I thought I might as well get beaten up with my clothes on. They all had their shiny caps set at the macho angle, down over their noses; they all wore big, solid boots. They were the 'lumps' – what you would class as prison security. They were getting red in the face because I wouldn't strip off. Well, fuck them. I was going to give as good as I got, or at least try to.

I went up to the biggest one I could find and bent as if to do my shoelaces. Then I came up with all the power I had and butted him in the face. I was kicking and punching. They were hitting me in the throat and up the arm and this went on for about five minutes. It seemed like an hour. I felt my bones being crushed and blood splattering. They all started punching me at the same time – the 'chickening up' I told you about. That's what they class it in the prison service. It really means beating all kinds of shit out of you, trying to tear you into little pieces like fricassee chicken. Lots of the screws had studded leather shoes and a load of these giant clogs of feet were coming at me, violently thumping into me time and time again. They didn't put the straightjacket on so I thought that was it; I'd had a touch and it was all over.

I was lying on the floor feeling sorry for myself, having had the fuck kicked out of me. I thought it was all over and I was just trying to get my strength back. There was a concrete slab which was cemented in – with a plastic sheet it was meant to be a bed – next to me on the floor. Ten minutes went by and I heard the footsteps again. I'd just stood up, the door was flung open and a mattress came through the door with the screws protected behind it. They fucking rushed at me full tilt and I was smashed against the back wall with this mattress. And all these big bastards began to beat the shit out of me again. I managed to try and protect my privates. Lucky for me, where I'd landed was bang in the middle of the mattress. They were trying to punch me in the head and punch me all over but I was getting some protection from the mattress.

Except for my left leg. I felt this pain. I've never felt anything like it. A screw had got his truncheon and batted my ankle and knee with it. After about a minute that seemed like forever, they all fucked off. My ankle was swelling as I watched it. I really felt like that was one hell of a fucking kicking. I'd never been kicked around like that before. It really was serious. I had always been fit and that saved my life. If I had not been superfit I would not have survived. They would have said I went insane and they had to fight me to subdue me. They didn't care about the consequences. They all had the bloodlust.

Me, I had blood pumping out of me. I felt my eye was going to come popping out. I thought my whole body was broken. I was fuming, furious with them. I'd never been so angry, so desperate to kick off. All I could think of was that I was going to be down that solitary area, away from the rest of the inmates, for months; they'd locked me back in the box and an hour – I think it was an hour but it could have been longer – went by.

Then the door opened and it was a Paki doctor. He said to me, 'What is the matter? What is the matter?' My ankle was like a balloon, I was soaked in blood, and my face looked like a pulverised pumpkin. The doctor said to the screw escorting him, 'There's nothing wrong with him.' I said, 'Nothing wrong!' I tried to hit out at him and I spat blood right in his fucking face. The screws all ran in and that was it. Another 'chickening you up' session. That was my first few hours at Wandsworth Prison. It didn't get better. I had lost about six months' remission.

My mum kept coming up and seeing me and as I was a top-security prisoner the visits were always behind glass. You've got a big glass partition with little holes drilled in it and you talk through that. My mum or other visitors – a maximum of three at a time – always seemed so far away for there was never any contact, nothing tactile.

Eventually, I got back on the wing and, fuck me, what do they do? They put me in with three Hell's Angels. Now my leg has healed up, I'm as good as gold but it's all a problem. When I walked back into 'society' I thought 'It's nice to be back on a wing' after being down on the block all that time. It had been like solitary – I knew no fucker.

Well, the Hell's Angels didn't exactly roll out the red carpet. It was a four-up cell but one of their mates had been nicked and gone off the wing and the nasty bastards running the place had replaced him with me. When I went in I thought I'd make the most of it and said, 'Hello boys.' Straight away this giant Hell's Angel, much bigger than me and wearing horrible corkscrew hair, came up and said, 'We don't want you in the cell, mate, you've got to get out, right? We've got a mate and we want him back in the cell.' I said to him, 'Fair enough, I don't want to be here either.' So straight away there's a bad atmosphere between me and these three Hell's Angels.

At night they've got the candles out and they're playing cards and talking away – it's got to about 1am in the morning. I said, 'What's going to happen, lads? Is this going to go on all fucking night?' They turned and said to me, 'If you don't like it, then go and fuck off like we told you to.' They were being right nasty. I had just come out of the choker and I'm thinking, 'I don't need this.' I thought that if I were to start, I was going to get a kicking off these Hell's Angels.

The next morning, I tried to get switched but, because I'd just come out of the block for assaulting screws, they didn't want to help me out at all. The message was clear: you, bastard, have to stay where you are. I did and it got really nasty – the Angels wanted me out of their heaven. And I had no allies – no one in Wandsworth knew me but as the days went on I got some 'All right, mate?' greetings from some of the others. It was getting round that I'd been down the block and I stood my own with the screws. I started getting a name in the prison system.

I tried again to change cells. I told them that if I didn't get a move it was going to go seriously off and people were going to get hurt. Someone made a decision and a screw told me: 'Right, get your kit and go down there.' When I went to get my stuff these Angels started abusing me. A blond-haired one with a broken nose had a hard chair and was threatening me with it. I went off but then I thought, 'I can't let these cunts get away with this.'

I went back and it was just the great big one with corkscrew hair. I went to him: 'Not so fucking mouthy now you're on your own, are you?' He came running at me like a big bear. He was about three or four stone heavier than me. As he ran, he grabbed me in a bear hug. But one of my arms was free. I went 'bang' with my fist, straight into his big, ugly mug. I felt a squelch. I had him round the neck with my arm, tightening my hold all the time. And I had my teeth in the side of his face, using it, gnawing it, like it was a big, juicy hamburger.

I had grabbed his hair and I was biting and pulling – and then the screws were on us. What a bunch of morons. They had no idea. It was like a sports day tug-of-war. First they had me around the body and then they grabbed corkscrew hair. They were pulling us apart. Yet, my teeth were stuck in his face. But the screws pulled and pulled and as they burst us apart a great big lump came right out of his face. I felt I had a lump of sponge in my mouth. I spat it out. Corkscrew needed about 30 stitches in his face.

The screws kept saying to me, 'You're nothing but trouble.' I was down the block for another three months, doing my time solo. I had the other cons' respect by then. I heard on the grapevine that corkscrew and his mates wanted and were planning revenge. When I got back on the block they were going to have me. Properly, they boasted. They were going to do this to me, that to me, I'd be singing soprano.

When I was back on the block, I was determined to sort it out immediately. I didn't want to be looking over my shoulder around the clock. Within, hours I got my chance in the canteen. The blond Angel, the one who had fancied knocking me around with a chair, was in the dinner queue. He didn't even have a notion I was back on the wing.

I had a razor which I'd got off one of the other cons; it had been smuggled in to him and he loaned me it for a bit of tobacco. I ran my thumb over the blade and it was sharp. I walked smartly up to blondie and I gave him a striping. I crisscrossed his face with the razor and he dropped to the floor, his hands and arms up to his face, yelling his head off. I never, ever had trouble with the Hell's Angels again.

The screws went ballistic. How had I got the razor? There were questions and enquiries but I was down the block again. They kept me locked up there for two years. A lot of it was down the block. My life was up and down blocks. It was a big, fast, fucking horrible, fucking awful gaff. They ran it like a military camp: if you stepped out of line they beat the shit out of you. But they were always a little bit wary of me because I'd had the big tear-up with them. One of the screws told his mate: 'Watch him – he thinks he's some kind of gladiator. He'll fight anything.'

From then on, it seemed, I was the big problem for the prison system. And I was going to be in it for some time. The next time I stood in the dock it was at the Central Criminal Court in London, at the Old Bailey.

Gladiator? I was a sitting target for the law.

CHAPTER SEVEN

RETRIBUTION

'I'VE LIVED MUCH OF MY LIFE IN A WORLD
POPULATED BY MADMEN AND TERRORISTS. MY
LAST CELLMATE IN 2002 WAS A MEMBER OF THE
TALIBAN. HE WAS A NICE FELLA.'

VICTOR DARK, 2003

I didn't win a get-out-of-jail card for my appearance at the Old Bailey. I went directly there from Wandsworth nick. While I had been inside for the street stabbing, the Old Bill had been furiously investigating the armed robberies we'd been doing all over London. That action, all those heavy bits of work, had become an increasing embarrassment to the braided-up cozzers and the pressure had been applied from high up. There was a size-ten boot up a lot of cozzers' arses.

Naturally, that kicking went all the way down to the streets and all my suspicions that we were being set up were proved true. I was well and truly grassed up. The cozzers had the goods on me – I had no choice but to plead guilty. Any other plea would just have got me more time for no reason. I knew the risks – I was about to pay the price. Handsomely.

On 25 July 1980, the system hammered me back for the sledgehammer gang spree. On paper, when I look at it now, they sentenced me to 96 years in prison! That's the arithmetic of it, 12 years times eight counts. Nearly a ton of years in jail. I was 23 years old.

These were the charges and the sentences:

1   *ROBBERY: 12 YEARS.*
2   *CARRYING FIREARMS WITH INTENT*
     TO COMMIT ROBBERY: 12 YEARS.
3   *ROBBERY: 12 YEARS.*
4   *CARRYING FIREARMS WITH INTENT*
     TO COMMIT ROBBERY: 12 YEARS.
5   *ROBBERY: 12 YEARS.*
6   *CARRYING FIREARMS WITH INTENT*
     TO COMMIT ROBBERY: 12 YEARS.
7   *ROBBERY: 12 YEARS.*
8   *CARRYING FIREARMS WITH INTENT*
     TO COMMIT ROBBERY: 12 YEARS.

It was all to run concurrent, so it came down to a twelve spot, but what a record it was. As it turned out, with stabbing sentence overlapping, I served eight years, five months and three weeks. My prison experience had been like kindergarten until then. My education was just beginning. And it wasn't all about violence and the cons, it was about the prison system which caused so much unnecessary hardship, depravity and death. Some men could not survive and took the easy way out by killing themselves. I saw some evil messes during my times inside.

Yet I rebelled all the time. I never asked for parole in all the years I was inside. I never asked for mercy. They could do their worst to me and I just came back. Yes, I buckled sometimes but no one ever saw that. If I had doubts and fears I hid them from all but myself and then I conquered them. Don't let the bastards grind you down – that's what should be on my tombstone. As it turned out, as a young man, I got a soft start. I was moved to Maidstone in Kent and didn't know until later what a lucky touch that was. Maidstone was quite an easy ride, not really one of those nasty prisons. It was a place for geezers like me who had been banged up for a long time. There were showers at each level and even the canteen wasn't bad. They kept the sex offenders in a different wing – it was called the Thanet Wing but to the cons it was the 'nonce wing' – so that stopped some trouble. It was an old jail – they used to hang people – but if I was ever comfortable being locked up, it was at Maidstone. We used to watch that Ronnie Barker series *Porridge* and get a right laugh. That Scots actor, Fulton McKay, who played the chief screw, had me in stitches. He was about as threatening as an ice cream compared to the real thing. I didn't want to be kicked out of Maidstone, so I towed the line. I used the gym, did my training and just gone with it.

Still, there were always people making mischief. There was a geezer – I can only call him Bobby – who would smash up other people's cells. He crashed up my cell and broke his own radio to make me think we had some hooligan about the place. Bobby tried to grass up my mate for it but that just provoked more trouble. I ended up bashing him up with an iron bar but I scraped out of trouble on that. My life inside prison was all ducking and diving – and surviving. At times, it was so claustrophobic I felt the walls were closing in on me, that the cells and the corridors were getting smaller. I just wanted to stretch my body, feel free, which of course was the last thing I was. I've seen men physically shrivel up in prison, get grey and white-haired in a matter of weeks. And, if you are banged up nearly all day every day, there is that jailhouse pallor that makes you really look like death, as though you are about to pop your clogs.

It's no wonder prison is full of suicides. I saw the results of some of them and even with all my experience with violence it was unsettling. Probably, I think, because it was so unnecessary. A geezer we called Taffy was my first suicide. Taffy was inside, recommended for a 20 stretch, for some Satan-inspired, heavy bit of work, but he seemed normal enough to all of us. He got on with doing his time and didn't bother anyone. We didn't know his brain was rattling around as though it had a .22 bullet in it. One day, when Taffy did not show from his cell, a screw we called Harry Worth, for he bumbled about all the time like the guy on the old telly show, shouted out for help. Taffy had blocked the cell door and I tried to help this Harry get into it. I shouted, 'Taff, open the door,' louder and louder.

Nothing happened. I went round with a stepladder with this screw and looked through the window and all I could see was this bit of wire strapped to the bars. As I looked down the wire, I could see a white geezer with long black hair. I said to the screw that something was seriously wrong and we went back and eventually got through the door. When we did, the screw was sick all down the back of my jeans. Taff had hung himself with a guitar string.

The wire had cut through his neck and half-decapitated him. Blood had sprayed everywhere. The screw was being sick again – it was one of most horrendous suicides I ever saw in jail. Taff had nearly chopped his own head off which was pretty remarkable.

There was a really nice fella called Paul who I liked a lot and he topped himself as well. He had been nicked for drugs; he was Scottish and looked like a popstar and was very brash and fun. He couldn't take prison. He hung himself – for him, there was no alternative. To this day I think of Paul and the people who have killed themselves in prison. It's a very sad place to be. Cons could be out all day long but, once they're banged up behind that door, they take all their worries and everything with them. They're locked up with their personal horrors and concerns and that's the hard part, that's when it plays dangerous games with the mind.

They need to spend money on changing prisons. Youngsters should not be allowed to hang themselves from bars. At the moment, they can knot sheets or shoelaces on the bars and top themselves; they could make windows lower, make it as hard as they can to stop the young kids from hanging themselves. I think people should be allowed more time out, to get more exercise, because when people are outside their cells they are not as liable to think of suicide. Suicides are very weird and come out the blue. You can't really put your finger on it but you can see the hallmarks of someone who is actually going to commit the suicide but you can never be sure. Some you can see, their wife has left them and they are acting strange. They don't want to talk to anyone. You can usually tell by their eyes. Very watery eyes. A mist over their eyes, like glass. If someone is depressed, you can look at their eyes. You can always tell.

They could help sort it by releasing more people on to the landings and watching them there: it wouldn't be so suffocating. But they won't. In every jail I've ever been in there's always the complaints about shortage of staff. I can understand that – what kind of person wants to watch over caged men? What mentality is that?

Prison is a dog-eat-dog world and you've got to be tough to survive. Obviously you see a lot of gays, although, to my surprise, there's more of that up north, with all these hairy bastards. When I first went in, it was a bit of a shock to me because they were holding hands and behaving like, well, a bunch of queers. Not that it made much difference at Maidstone because there most of their antics went on behind doors.

Maidstone was my graduating prison, where I learned the ropes, learned to do time. I won the prison's mile race, which I was proud of. I did it in just under five minutes which wasn't a bad time for me. I was superfit then. I held the record for the 20-kilo sit-up. I did 500 sit-ups straight off with a 20-kilo weight and I did about 800 with a 15-kilo weight, which is placed behind your neck instead of your hands. It's on the record books at Maidstone and I don't think it's ever been beaten. I got my gold badge in power lifting. We were one of the top prison weight-lifting power teams in Maidstone and in the country. In competitions, we did a 137 1/2 bench, a 245 squat and a 265 dead-lift. I only weighed 79kg. I got involved with a lot of that, it took my mind off the clock which always goes so slow when you're inside. Outside the times roars away with you, inside I felt like the Count of Monte Cristo, locked up forever. And, of course, I was.

You can take all the shit and let the screws run your life inside – it's called brown-nosing. That means you are a right fucking screws' boy. You get through it with no trouble and the screws looking out for you but you lose your dignity as a man. Yet, if you stick up for yourself, they provoke you. Well, let's put it this way, they fucking provoked.

I've spent much of my life behind bars and most of it as a Category 'A' or double 'A' prisoner – the ratings they give terrorists and the like. When I came out on remand after a dreadful caper in the summer of 2002, which I'll give you the inside story on later, I was one of a few geezers released back into society and still rated as a double 'A'. Kenny Noye was the first one. Kenny got life for the road-rage killing of Stephen Cameron in 2000, but when he got out on an earlier charge he was still a double 'A'. It's an exclusive club. I've served time in most of Britain's nicks, often doing stretches in the same one a couple of times, often the dispersal prisons which only take Category 'A's. They're the most secure units in England.

The thought of freedom kept me going through it all. It was all about positive thinking: the power of the mind. Especially when you are locked up down a segregation unit; a 'segs' keeps you apart from the rest of the prison population. If you haven't got a strong mind, you're fucked; that's what happens, simple as that.

I worked on a routine. It's all in the mind. I know it sounds stupid but it's things like having a hair-cut every week to keep it short and tidy, going to the gym every day, cleaning your cell, reading books. If I could not go to the gym because I was banged up I'd try to write and to learn something.

You've got to get some sort of regime going to pass the day. That's what it's all about and trying to fill your days up so you don't get bored. The horrors are the long stretches, when you are up for years and years inside. Take a 15-year sentence: you do ten years out of that, it becomes very, very hard because you worked through the first two or three years and, all of a sudden, it seems, you get the 'stagnant' part which is the three, four, five, six, seven, eight years that seem to be never ending. With the last couple of years you can see the end of it and it's easier.

I can't think of any other circumstances where you are quite literally just wishing your life away. You can't wait for your life to get past that ten years. I talked to lots of inmates about it. You know there's 365 days in a year and there's ten years of them. You feel despair. You wonder if you are ever going to get out.

When I was into the fourth year of my first big sentence it was a struggle. It was very hard. I used to ask for calmers to keep my rages down. I felt very angry, and I wanted to explode so I was got on these calmers. It was like Valium and it kept me mellow. Or, shall I say, mellower. Often, I still felt I wanted to knock out all the screws. Drugs can only do so much for your personality.

There was always the boredom and it's funny what you

can find to do with lots of spare time. My father had big earlobes and I got big ears from him. When long hair was fashionable it was OK but I never liked long hair – it was something for the other fella to grab hold of and no good in karate class. So I had short hair – and ears I hated. In Maidstone, I decided to change that.

I performed cosmetic surgery on my ears. With a pair of nail clippers. Clip, clip, clip, I went, and the job was done.

As I wrote, I've always been into martial arts – the no pain, no gain type of thing. I'm smothered in tattoos: legs, arms, body, inside my lips, and all that never bothered me, never hurt. I have always had a high pain threshold. I have been very lucky that I can block out pain. Pain is just a thing in your mind. The only pain you can't block out is emotional: pain as in a broken heart over a love affair. Pain like someone sticking a huge fucking knife through your hand can be dealt with.

I was reading these books about African tribes and how they put big things through their earlobes and their lips and all that. I thought, if they can do it, then I can do it. One day I was cutting my nails and thought I'd try trimming up my ear. I chopped most of it off, the fleshy stuff.

It came off really easily on the left one but I couldn't get the right one trimmed up so I called this Kenny into my cell. I said to him, 'Ken, do us a favour, help me with this.' He walked into my cell and saw all this blood everywhere and I said, 'You couldn't chop this unsightly bit of my ear off? I can't get to it properly.' He went out of the cell like a rocket. It went around the prison what I'd done.

I kept a big lump of earlobe which was about as big as the end of my thumb. I had it in a bit of tissue paper. The blood was spurting out. I remember thinking the blood was very thin but it was flowing well. To stop the bleeding, I put a cigarette paper and that Bonjela stuff, the toothache painkiller gel, on it. That night I put some more stuff on it and thought that if I didn't wake up in the morning, then I didn't wake up in the morning. Sure enough, I did and it wasn't too sore. I was in a good mood – I'd done quite a neat job.

The next day I was up for a laugh. We were all in the dinner queue and I said: 'I've got a bit more meat for the pie!'

With that, I whacked down the bloodied flesh on the canteen counter. The faces! Some of them didn't know whether to laugh or scream. At first, some of them though I'd cut some fella up but then they saw my ears.

I was called into the office and they asked me if I was all right. I said I was fine, prettier than ever. They sent me to the prison hospital and when I got there the screw said to me, 'What have you been doing? Have you been in some kind of a fight, Vic?' I said that I had big earlobes and had chopped them off. The screw nearly fell over. He couldn't believe it.

A week later and they've got me in Walton, the funny-farm prison facility. I was there for about three weeks so they could find out if I was off my head. I was interviewed by these three doctors. They looked at me and asked: 'What's the time?' There was a big clock behind them reading 4.05pm. I told them the time. I don't know if they were happy I could do that or not. Probably not.

One doctor who seemed to be the boss man asked me: 'If you would chop your own earlobes off what would you do to a fellow human being?'

I thought: 'I must be careful here or they are going to section me off – put me in a nutter's farm like Rampton or Broadmoor.' I said to him that it was just vanity. All I wanted to do, I told him, was make myself look better. I told him I always liked short hair and I couldn't have it because of my ears. I convinced them that it was nothing, just taking a bit of flesh off. I got moved to Strangeways, and then back to Maidstone. Me and my little ears.

Later, in another nick, I had to do some more creative surgery on my ears. With all the karate and the kick-boxing, the top of my ears had grown; I had got thick ears like a rugby player. I took the top off them both and got a neat line. I did my own plastic surgery. I know it sounds crazy but it saved me about two grand in doctor's bills. That's one of the maddest things I've ever done but it kept me busy. I wasn't bored but no other con ever asked me to do surgery on them. I'd have been quite happy to do it. I like the sound of Doctor Dark, like someone from the Hammer horror movies: 'Doctor Dark will see you now ...'

I was always looking for something to take my mind off doing time and the nasty screws were always a good target. When I was in Wandsworth in the Seventies and Eighties there was this big, fat bastard who was always giving me trouble. I was working in the mailbag shop – yes, we sewed up mailbags, just like the cons do in those old black-and-white movies – and we worked with long needles. This arsehole screw spent all his time with his fat arse in a chair in a box overlooking us like an umpire at Wimbledon. If you weren't doing anything he would jump on you. That proper dog of a screw was always giving me the needle so I decided to give him some of his own. The needles were about four inches long and an eighth-of-an-inch thick.

We had balls of white wax, which we used to wax the string for the mailbags. I placed a needle, sharp end pointed up, in the wax and then stuck the wax ball on the screw's chair. The screw walked up and looked around, made sure we were busy and then went to sit down. As he sat down, he stood up again. I thought, 'Aw, fucking hell, he's seen the needle'. But he hadn't. He was looking around again and then he sat straight on this needle. It went straight up his arse. The screw jumped up out of his chair, the needle still stuck up his arse, and started to have a go at everyone. He was ranting and raving and with that a fight broke out.

The screw jumped down from his chair and ripped into

these geezers near to him. I sat at the workbench trying to look surprised – I couldn't laugh my head off because no one knew I had put the needle in the chair. He had to go to hospital and it was removed. It took about two hours to get this needle out of his arse. No one ever sussed it was me.

As I said, he was a proper dog that screw but not all of them are such bastards. When screws first come into the job, a lot of them mean well and they want to do their utmost to help you and all that. But, after a few years, they all get like the rest: very, very bitter. They don't trust you and don't like you. For screws, part of the job is being a two-faced cunt. There are some exceptions but very rare. There was one in Parkhurst who was generally a nice fella and he was the only one I ever encountered.

Our exchanges went:

'All right, Dark?'

'All right, Gov?'

That was it. It was them. And it was us. They worked for the system. They had a job to do. If they left me alone, I would leave them alone.

For a tiny percentage of the years spent inside, you can have good times in prison. It's not all bad. Another way of passing the time was getting pissed. Surprised? Well, inside you can get as drunk as any lord, as shit-faced as any free man, if you know how – or someone who knows how. I was a brewmaster, a master brewer. To this day I can make you a better drink than you'd get at the bar of any top hotel but, as I've heard it, that's not too much of a challenge. Let's just say I could match any fancy barman cocktail for cocktail. It was just that my equipment was possibly more rudimentary.

I made hooch in prison starting with the buckets we used to pee in. Obviously, I used to get clean ones! Let me give you the recipe – you can try this at home. It's safe but don't drive. Of course, on the outside you can buy the special ingredients at the shops. Me and the rest of the cons in the booze game had to rely on materials being smuggled in, or a little bit of imagination. The rest we could buy or snaffle inside.

My brew started with 2lbs of Tate & Lyle sugar, brewer's yeast from prison kitchens and a foot-high plastic jug of semi-hot water. I filled the jug almost to the top and put the brewer's yeast in. I let it all froth up, like beer froth on top, for about an hour. I then put the sugar in the bucket. Now, I added lukewarm water – it has to be lukewarm, if it's too hot it will kill the yeast. It must be kept nice and warm. I used to buy pure orange juice out of the canteen. You can add apples or oranges, any sort of fruit, but my brew used two or three cartons of pure orange juice. I used to joke that the technique was all in the stirring.

I stirred the mix carefully for the first day and then at regular intervals for about a week and gradually the yeast particles fell to the bottom. You get about a couple of inches of yeast at the bottom. The trick is to let it ferment slowly, not rush it, no matter how much you fancy a drink. We used to hide the hooch in lockers or, if we found somewhere within a prison where they never searched, we would stick it there. We'd put it in three or four black bin liners to try and contain the smell. There's a terrible stink making drink with yeast and keeping the smell down was the hard part. By about the sixth day, you take the bin liners off and you will see that the yeast, which is about an inch thick, has fallen to the bottom and the rest of it is the hooch. You strain the drink off into another bucket, leaving the sediment at the bottom. I used to strain it again through a towel. Before we went on the booze, I would add a spoonful of yeast back in the bucket and – 'Same again, Gov?' – start the bucket up for another batch.

That's when we toasted ourselves with what was as good as a vodka and orange. Delicious. I was a real brewmaster and had a prison reputation for it. I could make hooch that tasted better than some of the stuff in pubs today. I was that good. It is all to do with the yeast. If you get the yeast, kitchen yeast or brewer's yeast, you could make a nice drink. It was the absolute bollocks. It was as strong as fuck. It would blow my socks off. We would all get rotten drunk.

I used to have a puff of cannabis now and then but, as the years went on, it became very tight. What the authorities did was pushed all the silly bastards who were having a bit of puff, which never hurt anyone, on to the smack. The silly fuckers kick-started a heroin craze in the prison system. That daft cow Ann Widdecombe when she was at the Home Office. She brought in mandatory drug testing. The geezers who wanted to get high were not stupid. If they smoked puff it hung around in their systems for 28 days and they could end up with aggro they did not need. Smack comes out of people's systems in 24 hours – much, much faster, so the chances of failing a dope test are less. Smack makes sense, stupid! By being tough on puff the system got them on the junk which couldn't be so easily tested; the authorities didn't think it through, but they never do. All the system did was made a load of junkies. After about four years they became aware of it and it was ordered that if you got caught with cannabis the punishment would be half of that if you were caught with heroin. The authorities knew what had happened but too late; they pushed them on to smack and it's reflected on today's society. When the smack addicts got out they found much stronger heroin on the streets than they ever got inside and the result was a rash of overdoses. Who's the Labour bloke responsible now, Blunkett? I don't suppose whoever is in charge now gives a shit either.

There was never any credit for being your own man. I got some dogs that wanted to search my underpants. I was in a segregation unit at Brixton and this screw bellows out at me: 'Take your shorts rights off.' I stood there and shook them around me as you do and he said, 'Right off.' I wouldn't do it. Two days after a visit they want to check you have had nothing smuggled in – that screw and a couple of others came up to me. Happy boy barked again: 'Take your shorts off!' I said that if he got me a gown I'd happily agree to his request. I was polite as could be. He didn't like that and said, 'We're giving you a direct order to take your shorts off.' I went to him: 'You get me a gown and I'll take the shorts off.' A lot of screws turned up but I still refused until they gave me a gown. Screws! They have the mentality of baked beans: they wanted to go through this charade day after day.

So, I started shitting all my boxer shorts up. Every time the screw wanted my shorts off, I used to take my shorts off full of shit, and put them straight into his hand. His face, well you've never seen anything like it. He can't nick me for having dirty underpants. After that he did it about twice and that was it.

Shitting up the screws was part of the guerrilla warfare inside; there's always a way to skin a cat, get around things and make the screws as uncomfortable as possible. Apart from a real heavy going over, the screws hated being shitted up more than anything. It simply meant they had a bucket of shit thrown over them. What we did was pass the bucket around – have a shit whip round, the cons' equivalent of the church collection – and use it as ammunition. I've seen so many screws getting shitted up. They just don't like it. And I can't blame them but it's often what they deserve. If the cons were more sophisticated they'd drop flasks of shit on them – the mess would explode all over the place.

You get a flask, take the inside out, which is all glass, and fill it with shit and piss. It's glass and shit. The screws couldn't handle it. They could smell shit, and they would stand on the landing and think when the next fucking bomb was going to hit them. Dropped down the landing, it would just explode like a bomb. When it goes, it's shit everywhere! Nuclear! The screw does not like being shitted up.

If you punch them on the jaw they go off sick for three months, but if you shit them and they get it in their eyes and their mouths, then it degrades them. They do it to us, they pick their nose and put bogeys in our food, piss in our drinks and things like that, so we shitted the fucking dogs up. It was one way I managed to have control in prison.

There was a nice kid called Keith who was from Middlesbrough. He'd been in some heavy trouble – he got shot through his face and they cut him open and put a tube down to save his life – and wound up in Parkhurst. Now, the Isle of Wight is OK for some but when you're from up north, you want to be in nick close to the family. This Keith said to me, 'What's the best way to get out of here?' No contest, I said, but to shit a screw up. Keith got this bucket and there must have been ten of us or more and we had a whip round. There was this one screw, he really did think he was a special number: he had an immaculate shirt, gelled-back hair, thought he was a colonel or something, strutting about the place.

To entice the screw into the best position to be shitted up the trick was to ask them to open a door on the landing. Keith was in his cell, conned the screw to the top of the stairs and whooshhhhhh!!! A spectacular shitting up for the screw, who slid down the stairs on his back and landed at the back of the landing. We all knew him as 'Shithead' after that but Keith never saw him again. He was moved out of Parkhurst. What a staunch geezer.

Sometimes it was important that we prisoners were in charge of the asylum because the screws could be truly thick. At Whitemoor, there was a fire and about 40 screws were running around shouting about banging up, locking us all in our cells. There's a fire and they want to lock us in! I was having a drink with some of the lads and the screws came around shouting about banging up. I said, 'I ain't being banged up.' A screw told me to get behind the door and I said, 'What about that fire? You want me banged up?' I told him to fuck off. I said to him, 'If that fire comes over here, are you going to come and get me out, mate?' He looked blank. I went, 'Are ya?' He went, 'Point taken.'

Then, he said he was concerned and said to the other screws, 'Get them out of here.' All the cons were moved to a safe area – the cell doors got so fucking hot they were swelling up. It was a raging fire and if we'd let them bang us up we'd have been barbecued.

They hold on to their grudges in the prison system. Nobody hears about the cells being burned up, the tit for tat. I got moved around a lot for being a rebel. They had special jails for the really bad boys. On one move this screw said to me, 'You know where you're going, don't ya?' I went, 'Where's that then?' and he went, 'Lincoln.' He said, 'You know the reasons why, don't you?' I said, 'Tell me.' He said, 'If you step out of line, you'll get done ...'

When I got there, all the screws were lined up like a welcoming committee. I bet they were lined up for Jeffrey Archer – Lord Archer that is – when he got packed off there in September 2002, after being a bad boy on day release. I read his prison diaries – don't make me laugh. I've told you what prison is really like. Archer? He set himself up as a prison reformer: 'Hey, look at me, I'm doing a public service.' He didn't tell the world anything it didn't already know. Tosser.

Me? I never had a chance of champagne lunches and good times on the outside during my prison terms. I had to arrange drink, fun – and sex – on the inside. Don't get the wrong idea about the sex; I'll explain how I got my rocks off at Her Majesty's Pleasure. And it was a pleasure. You'll have to wait a little longer for the details.

When I went to Lincoln Prison the screws put me in a cell in one piece, they could clearly wait for a more convenient moment to kick the living shit out of me. The screws fucked off and I had a meet with the Governor. I hated the fucking Governor with his sideburns like a farmer's.

'What the fuck am I doing here?' I said.

'Don't you swear at me,' he snarled, and I asked him again what I was doing there. He went, 'Let's have a game.'

'Any game you want,' I said.

I was lucky, there were a lot of hard men in the jail and I knew most of them. We were our own force against the screws. When they served us food we threw it out of the cells saying it was shit. That was part of the confrontation. And they couldn't bash me in because there was a group of us standing together. It was like Spartacus and the gladiators. Together, as a unit, you can beat the bastards. And there had been so much trouble in the system that the Governor wanted some peace on the premises. They allowed us to go to the gym, to keep us quiet, because it was a controlled unit. We broke the back of it because we were so solid; they knew every time they undid that door that they were going to be attacked. They had to come up with some solutions to have peace with us. That's how good we were. I was lucky there. I had a hard core there, but if I had been there with another fucking ten wallies, I would have had my head kicked in. I did stand my ground with a lot of them so that's where I made my name in jail. For being staunch and saying, 'Fuck off.'

When I was in Frankland, they were bashing everyone up. They would march into cells and beat up geezers. There were two Cockneys there who had a row, one calling the other a grass. I knew the geezer being called a grass – he was nicked for the murder of a wealthy businessman – and his family. The noise went back and forward, I'm in the middle, and the fight starts. The guy mouthing off hits my mate, so I swept his legs away with a kick and gave him a crack on the head. Nothing too serious. The screws have seen it and they want to take me off the compound. A load of them rush in shouting, 'You've got to come with us.'

'Fuck off,' I said.

'You've got to come with us,' they said.

'I'll come after my exercise,' I said.

All of a sudden they jump me and about six mates. We steamed in and did a proper bang-up job of them. The screws just ran. They hadn't got control of the jail.

We took over Frankland. They couldn't do a thing. We were such a tight unit. We brought them to heel. They stopped all the beatings. We stood up to them. When you get armed robbers, we are the chaps and there is no way they were going to beat us up, we weren't going to have it. One against many and I'm fucked, but 20 of us against 300 of them, it evens up.

They moved me again. I got moved all the time.

The prison system tries to fuck your head up. They do it with the four-man DST teams who carry out 'special searches'. They come into your cell and the order is immediate: 'Strip search!' They try to make you squat – to see how weak you are – to see if you've got anything hidden up your arse. I would never squat. It should be illegal but it's part of the strip search this mob do. They take anything and everything in your cell apart – they are like storm troopers. They carry riot shields, like the ones you see in Ireland. They're all in black: black visors, black helmets, black shields and big boots with knee protectors and shin pads. They're done up like robots. They are the team that can suddenly appear and take you away.

It's done under the 'Good Order and Discipline' which they use against most people like myself whom they class as subversives. They can come to your cell at any moment of the day and say, 'We are placing you on good order and discipline which is Rule 43.' It's this rule that nonces go on, but Rule 43 also allows them to remove you from your cell and hold you in solitary for up to 28 days. It's a method for taking rebels our of the prison population. If they want to keep you down the chokey they just have you up before the Board of Visitors and time and time again you can get the 28 days.

I've known people be down the chokey for years. People like Warren Slaney who is a good friend of mine. They had him in a place called Wood Hill. They'd had him banged up for years. In 2002, he'd been down the segregation unit for two years. They've jumped on him on his visits. They took terrible liberties.

There was an Indian fella called Ram who protested his

innocence and got carted off. It annoys me because people protest their innocence, and for that they lock them up in the segregation units. They make their lives miserable. You can't even protest that you are innocent because, if you do, they'll put you down the segs. I felt sorry for Ram. He was in a street fight against a white man and it was self-defence and they put him away for life. Boy, did he suffer. I've seen people who are classed as hardcore prisoners, I won't mention their names 'cos it will just get them more aggravation, but my hat goes off to some very strong people. People like Kevin B and Charlie M and Charlie B, some very strong principled people who have stood up to the prison system. Fighting back is the only way to survive as a man.

I had to use my mind to get out of prison, to drift off into my imagination, my own world. There's a lot of crap written about the easy life in prison but that's about the white-collar bandits, the ones that rob millions and get duck-down pillows and, for all I know, special wanking facilities. People like Jeffrey Archer. But, like him, they're all wankers to begin with.

For the majority it is not easy. It was six years before I first got to use a payphone in the nick. You could use the prison phone to make a call once every two weeks and then, if you were really lucky, once a week. The visits were a help but always difficult. As I wrote earlier, you could have three people maximum to visit even if you were not top security, behind glass.

We 'A' men were treated differently. I was surrounded by screws for every visit. They corner you off and it's as if you are in a box, one at each corner of the table where you sit. You couldn't talk properly, especially to girlfriends, with six to eight men, all with serious attitude, around you. That's why long-term relationships virtually came to nil; the screws don't make for a romantic atmosphere. You can't say 'I love you'. You can't really have a touch or a feel in your relationship because there's all these people looking at you. 'A' men get the worst end of the stick. I was an 'A' for all my prison sentences and an 'AA' for eight and a half years.

As an 'A' man you get watched every hour and you have to have the light on because the rules dictate that the screws look through the peephole on the hour. It was a red light and all night long your light would be on from when you go to bed to early morning. If you can't sleep with a light on you've got serious problems. Your cell was always lighted. Someone was always checking. I was always on 'parade'. I imagine it was like being in a freak show, a curiosity.

You have to switch off from the outside world, disconnect yourself, when you're in prison. If you didn't, you'd go mad. It's not the sounds, the hubbub of prison, that gets you, but the cacophony of noise inside your head. If you thought about your girlfriend going down the pub every night, going round to her mate's house or going down clubs and meeting other fellas, you would send yourself round the bend. For you, time stops when the prison gates close and the cell door slams behind you.

You must sever all thoughts of the outside and say to yourself that what she's doing, she's doing. Inside prison, your personal identity fades and finally evaporates. You must just accept that another life is going on but it is in a parallel universe: it has nothing to do with you. If you can get through a prison sentence like that, you can get through anything. Nothing can be as terrible as that.

It is always about mental attitude. When you walk inside that prison, you must realise the only person who can do that prison sentence is you. You're the only person who can help you through it. You. Your family can help, but not enough. You're the only person who can physically get you through that prison sentence. You can't cry to no one, you can't talk to no one. You can't do nothing. You have to be the one to do it.

When you're actually down, and that door bangs, it's goodnight cruel world. You can think, 'Let me out of here!' but they won't – not until you have served your time. Every moment, second, minute and year of it.

Yes, I could have been another suicide, another prison statistic. At times I know I could have killed myself and not done the time, but I got through. I came out and I believe I came out much, much stronger. And wiser, but a little bit daunted by certain situations.

The mistake when you get out of prison is to forget what it was like, how bad it was. You mustn't forget what it's like. In prison you've got nothing. You've got one toothbrush, you've got your tooth powder. They used to make you pay for your own toothpaste out of the £3 a week you had to live on. £3 a week. When you're inside the best thing you can have is a pair of old, rotten jeans. I was told what to do all the time. What time I could eat, what time I could drink. I even had to ring a bell when I wanted to go for a shit. Now it's a bit better, toilets are in your cell.

When you come out you might have this, you might have that, and you forget about prison. But when you look around, you realise you've got a lot more than you've ever had. Sometimes you can forget it. That is one thing you mustn't do. I've done that and I've always regretted it – not the blagging, not the action, but the fact that what you're doing is making it possible for them to lock you up again.

Of course, when I was released near the end of 1987 from that first long stretch, I was well ready to prove my bones again. I was only 31. Spectacular action is what I wanted. I was a professional armed robber. What else could I be expected to do?

And I got employment, with some of my heaviest work ever. It was so extravagant I got decorated for it – with headlines.

CHAPTER EIGHT

THE BIG HEAT

'HE WAS FALLING EVERYWHERE
AFTER LOSING ALL THAT BLOOD, LIKE HE
WAS DRUNK. ONCE AGAIN, I HAD SECOND
THOUGHTS. I COULDN'T DO THAT.
I COULDN'T LEAVE HIM. I'D GOT TWO
GUNS ... I'D GET US OUT OF THERE.'

**VICTOR DARK, IN 2003, RECALLING THE
INFAMOUS PENTHOUSE RAID**

I was in back in my old stomping ground, living in Walthamstow, and taking my time – and some liberties – all over the East End. As soon as I got out of nick, I was approached about pieces of work, armed robberies and the like, but I wanted to get used to the outside world. And one of the major things prison time taught me was to be careful with people. What they're saying and what you're seeing don't always match the reality of situations.

I had gone down for the sledgehammer jobs because of being grassed up. The planning and execution of the work had always produced results and no problems. Yes, there's a little bit of luck involved but in that business chance is always a prime factor.

Boredom was my problem, even on the outside. I couldn't

settle down to much and I've never liked sitting around watching the telly or anything like that. I went to the gym and down several karate clubs. I was still superfit and I spent a lot of time with free weights and the kick-boxing. I hadn't been out of nick for many months when I took a day out to a little village called Runfold, near Farnham, in Surrey. There were a couple of nice clubs there: a disco and a jazz club.

For a bit of action, I got a shotgun and robbed them. There was only around £2,000 to be earned that day but it was good to be back at work. I suppose it is like an addiction – I needed the 'high' from work, from taking the chances, putting my life on the line. When they nicked me, the cozzers charged me with robbing the jazz club and *two* discos that night. When they read the charge sheet to me saying I'd robbed three clubs in one night I looked the cozzer in the eye and asked him: 'Who do you think I am? Fucking Superman?' That's all I said to him. I kept looking at this policeman, staring him in the eye, and he started playing with his tie and being really uncomfortable. Finally, they just done me with the armed robbery of the jazz club and one disco.

The great thing with these little jobs was I only had myself to worry about. For other jobs I had a couple fellas I did some work with. This and other work caught up with me eventually, but then, even after the prison stretch, I felt invincible.

I was so blasé about it that one Sunday afternoon – it was raining and I was fed up – I took off and robbed a place. Also, I could always get work as a bouncer at a disco or a club and that let me see what was going on, what was about, and also gave me an alibi for being at other places. If I was going to do a bit of work, maybe rough up someone or shoot a fella in the legs to frighten him up, the bouncer's job allowed me to sneak off, do the business and then be straight back on the door. There was so much going on at the clubs that nobody ever noticed me vanishing to do my moonlighting, if that's what I can call it.

The robberies were something else to do, a little business to free my nervous energy. And I was impatient then, I didn't have the sense to wait things out. I was in that frame of mind when I was approached about an enterprise involving the 'Penthouse', a flashy nightclub in High Road, Ilford. The two people I was grafting with were away on holiday – they could afford it! – and without them around I was anxious for some action.

The Penthouse was managed by a fella called David and he wasn't well liked. Maybe that's why the people who approached me wanted his club robbed. I never asked that question – it seemed like good takings, a bit of a challenge and an adventure. The unspoken message to me was that if Dave got slapped around a little everybody would be happy.

But primarily it was an armed robbery and I had to look on it as a military sort of objective, as I always had. First, I needed another pair of hands, and I recruited this mate of mine who I'll call Steve. Steve was a curly-haired geezer: tall and fit, well experienced in the business and always up to take a chance. I felt I could rely on him, we would watch each other's back throughout the work on the Penthouse. I felt confident about that.

The Penthouse closed around 2.30am. Lots of the punters were from local restaurants and pubs that shut up a couple of hours earlier. It was the last weekend of September 1988, and we planned to do the place over in the early hours of the Sunday when nearly all the takings would be in. We'd nicked a Vauxhall car, some naff model, a Jerry Springer – a 'ringer' – and that afternoon I went out to buy the robbery kit. My normal stuff was round some geezer's house and I didn't want to disturb him, or draw attention to what I was up to.

At about 4pm that Saturday I'd bought two balaclavas, two rucksacks and two boilersuits with red piping from an Army & Navy store in Manor Park. I paid cash. Then I realised I didn't have a proper watch for a night job, one that would light up with the time. At the time I had this big Rottweiler called Bono and he had slipped in the bedroom and eaten my work watch, all the workings and most of the strap. I kept expecting Bono to go tick-tock like that alligator in *Peter Pan*.

I got this new work watch, which had a button that flashed up the time in the dark. It was important because I had the timing worked out in seconds. That Saturday night I picked up two .38 revolvers. One was a short-nose revolver which was a Canadian Police Special and the other was a long-nose revolver. The guns were to help more than I imagined.

I planned to be at the club at 1am on the Sunday and phoned Steve to meet me in Walthamstow at 12.30am. He came round my house in a taxi and that's what did him the best turn that night. No one knew Steve was working with me, because he wasn't the geezer I was regularly grafting with. It was a horrible night, pissing down with rain. The Penthouse had a regular set of bouncers, three or four experienced blokes who did a professional search of people going in the main entrance. The punters went in and up a lift and it was when they came out of the lift that the bouncers 'greeted' them. A nice ambient start to the evening!

And a no entry for me. There was no way I was going to smuggle all my gear, the rucksacks, the guns and bits and pieces, through that sort of security.

But I had fixed all that with someone working in the Penthouse. The plan was to get inside through the back doors, which would be opened from the inside at exactly 1am, and then wait until all the punters had left. Only then would we show ourselves and do the business. The idea was to let us out, tie the fellas up, take the money and go. The escape had also been thought out. After the place was empty a security man padlocked and chained the doors including the getaway. I knew all about that and the inside boy had left bulkcutters in the box room for me.

We drove to the Penthouse with jackets and trousers over our boilersuits and parked in position in a quiet lane at the rear of the club. We stripped down to the boilersuits, checked out our gear and, looking like a couple of SAS men, right on the hour, as planned, we were let into the club. We were taken up the back stairs, through the exits and into a box room just outside the kitchen area.

It was easy. Too easy, as it turned out. Not one of those inside boys had the sense to tell me about the entertainment that night: there was a Caribbean party on one side of the club and a normal discotheque on the other. It was an especially big party night for them.

We were in this box room waiting for the signal – three bangs on the door to alert us that all the punters had left and there were only Dave and his helpers, about eight geezers, still in the club with their takings. All we could hear was throbbing music. It was hot in this box room next to the kitchen. I kept flashing on the light of the new watch and, finally, it read 2.30am. It was time for everyone to leave. It looked like the plan was going well. I wanted all of them out of the way, for a police Panda car, sitting ten floors beneath, always waited outside the Penthouse to make sure there was no trouble. With the punters off the premises, the Panda car would be off on its rounds. I'd checked it in previous weeks and that was what always happened.

Suddenly, the music stopped. But it was 2.45am. What was going on? The time ticked away slowly, and at 3am there's a knock on the door. But my inside man wants time to get off the premises before we go into action. I gave him 15 minutes. At 3.15am we started our business.

I marched out and took a left down the corridor and into a room. I was carrying a bottle of ammonia in my left and a .38 in my right. If you squirt someone with ammonia it'll take them right out of the game. If it gets in your eyes you can't see anything. About 30 faces were looking at me. I shouted at them to get down but they just looked at me. I don't know who was more shocked. I shouted again: 'Get down on the fucking floor!' The punters should have been well gone. There was a big, tall guy who they were calling Omar who hovered near me. I said to everyone again to get down on the floor and no one seemed to take any notice.

I moved my gun from my right hand into my left hand. I punched this black geezer Omar, who's about 6 foot 3, and he went straight down, right on his back. He just sort of lay there, and I thought, 'Fucking hell, that's a good punch.' I was quite proud of that. The rest of them got the message and they all got down on the floor.

One woman had seen me appear with the gun and had run off. Out of the corner of my eye I saw a guy with a black shirt and red tie – a bouncer. I hit him with my elbow and he went straight down. Then, I turned my attention to the other half of the room, where the disco had been. Then that's when I took the left into the disco. It was a mess. Steve, stupid Steve, was listening to a geezer shouting at him: 'Do you know there's security on the premises, do you know what you're doing?'

Steve should have just banged the guy out of it and got on with the job of ripping out the phones and getting to the money in the office. But, not doing his job properly, he was letting him talk to him. It was hopeless. In those moments we should have been operating, instead this geezer, who turns out to be David, is screaming for security.

I had gone past Steve and David and into the disco part. There was about another 30, 35 people in there. I got them all lying down on the floor. I went back up to the top of dance floor and was met by another crowd of punters. They started walking towards me. I gave this front runner a karate kick in the chest which floored him.

People started running all over the place, panicked and trying to get out of any trouble but they all ended up on one side of the room. I was swearing and shouting and wondering what to do: there were about 100 people in the place. I turned round and all of a sudden Steve, who is dressed exactly the same as me, with a blue rucksack, blue boilersuit, is beside me saying 'All right'. I thought Steve had got the money, that everything was OK.

I kept to the plan. I ran past Steve as I'd promised to give David a clump for the people who set this thing up for me.

I walked up to this David and held the gun to the centre of his head. At that moment, I heard that stupid cunt Steve say, 'Come on, Vic.' In astonishment at him saying my name, I looked around, as anyone would.

David had bottle and he grabbed the gun. He pulled it to the left-hand side, dragging it down really fast. I pulled the trigger and part of his thumb blew off.

He let go of the gun and I thought, 'You cunt.' I shot him another couple of times. I thought I shot him three times in the stomach but I didn't. One bullet went through his abdomen, one blew a hole through his hand and another went straight through his arm.

I wasn't meant to shoot him like that. It wasn't supposed to happen like that. David fell on the floor and I went back to Steve and tried to stay calm with him, and said, 'Have you got the money yet?' He hadn't. And he didn't have the keys to the office where the cash was. I went back to David, gave him the evil and coldly said to him, 'Right, give me the fucking keys.' The geezer had been shot proper and was rolling around on the floor. I wasn't getting anywhere with him.

I turned round and walked back and realised that Steve had been shot. How the fuck …? I just did not have a clue at that moment but in that fracas with David, when the gun had pulled down and David was trying to aim it at me, a bullet had gone past me and caught Steve. It had hit him in the arm and then gone right through his body and out the back.

There is bedlam. It was like a madhouse. There's people screaming and gunsmoke everywhere. The lights are flashing. The noise is horrendous.

I ran over to Steve. He was holding his hand, which blood was pumping through, spurting out through his fingers. The bullet had hit a main artery. As I grabbed him he dropped his gun. I picked it up. I now had my own two guns back and I shoved them in my pockets and hoisted Steve across my shoulder.

I followed our escape plan but the chain and the padlock on the back doors were so big there was no way the bulkcutters could do the job. I pulled one of the guns. I was going to shoot the chain off. But it was a metal door and, if I had fired at it, the bullets would have ricocheted and hit me. I couldn't fire the lock off. I was cursing and thinking and there was only one way to go – back to where we'd been. There's pandemonium inside and police sirens in the streets below. I only had one option – to run down the ten flights of stairs with Steve on my back and try and fight my way through the cozzers. I knew they'd be armed. From the top floor I could see all the people milling around in the street – and all the cozzers.

The getaway was prepared. All I had to do was take off the boilersuit and the balaclava, dump the guns and in my street clothes walk out with all the others trying to escape the chaos and violence. If I left Steve I had a very good chance. My mind was racing very, very fast and I didn't know what to do. I had my opportunity now but did I leave Steve or not? Imagine what was going through my mind: 'If I take these off, dump the guns, I could just walk out of here with the crowd and no one will be any the wiser.'

With Steve being shot, there was nothing I could do. I had to take him with me. It turned out to be the biggest mistake of my life. He turned out to be a dog. I should have put a bullet in his brain and left it at that. But, I had a strong, principled life and so I decided to get hold of him and try to help him downstairs. In the kitchen it was all tiled and the blood was everywhere. Squirts of blood kept splashing out.

And the faster I ran down the stairs with him, the quicker the blood was pumping out. It was pouring out of him. There were sprays of blood everywhere. All up the walls from Steve where the artery in his arm was punctured.

I had Steve off my shoulder and was trying to help him down the stairs with my arms around him. But he was falling everywhere after losing all that blood, like he was drunk. Once again, I had second thoughts. But I couldn't do that. I couldn't leave him. There was blood dripping all down the back of my boilersuit. I'm in a mess with it all. I put the ammonia back in my top boilersuit pocket and realised that the bullets I had there had fallen out when I kicked the geezer in the chest.

I had the two guns in one hand, then in my right, and then in my left, and all the time trying to cope with Steve's body which is getting more and more of a dead weight. He might even have been dead but I had no time to check at that point for as I reached the bottom of the stairs there was a cry: 'That's them, that's them.'

I raised a gun and said, 'Don't fucking move.' They all just stood there. Everyone was looking at me. I shouted again, 'Stand back, or I'll shoot.' They stayed put, like statues.

My first instinct was to get Steve to the getaway car and get the fuck out of there. I went about 50 yards with Steve and we got to the top of a hill, a natural moment to look behind. There were police cars coming up behind me. There were lots of cozzer cars in the area – cars keeping a watch on the nightclubs. I was almost at our car but the police were coming towards us. Just as I got to the getaway car a police car pulled right up at us. I had the revolvers in my hands; the cozzers could see that.

I put Steve on the ground and the cozzer couldn't believe it when I ran over to his car and grabbed him out of the motor. As I turned with the cozzer all the other cars were circling, easing towards me. As the policeman was standing by the side of the police car I raised my guns and pointed to the policeman and shouted, 'Go back, go back.' There was a Montego, a Metro and another car and they all started reversing. They were all marked police cars.

I chucked the cozzer back in the car and looked at Steve. He was bleeding but alive. I didn't have time to be Dr Kildare so I chucked him in the back of the Panda car. I got in the front of the car.

Where do we go? I don't want to go anywhere near where I live. Right? Left? Anywhere? I shout at the cozzer (he turns out to be PC Peter Coult, PC 191), 'DRIVE!' He puts his foot down. I don't know where I am. I am totally fucking lost! It's a big chase. I'm in a police car with other police cars chasing us. We go through red traffic lights, down Seven Kings. I didn't think there was any way I was going to get away. We were doing 60 to 70mph. I picked the gun up and said to the policeman, 'Get the fucking units to back off.'

With that, he got on his radio and broadcast: 'Units, units, back off.' All the units started to fall away.

With that, the gun's gone off. I think my adrenalin was pumping so fast I pulled the trigger without realising what I was doing. The gun blew the window out of the side of the police car. The policeman is shitting himself. He had residue on his head. That's gunpowder. That's how close it was. It just whistled past his head. It hit the back of his neck. The gun had just gone off. No one would have believed me if the bullet had gone through his brainbox. They would have just said I killed him. I would have got locked up forever, got 30 recommended. I probably would have topped myself – no way would I have done 30 years in jail.

There's that gunpowder smell and the cozzer's still driving. All the units have backed off and we take a left and down into a cul-de-sac. I don't know what the fuck to do.

I pulled the policeman out of the car, and we looked at each other. I was going to put him in the boot, but he's in a Metro and I can't do that. I looked at my mate and for the first time I thought that if I knock that cozzer off and nut Steve off no one is going to know me.

For a split second a bit of a madness came over me, but I knew I couldn't do that. Principles, principles!! I decided to dump the Panda car, which was soaked in blood. I told the policeman to take Steve out and I made him carry him. He had blood over his shirt as we were running down this alleyway, it was a quick walk, and I had the gun behind the policeman carrying Steve. We took a right and then came out on a road in Romford.

We stopped at the first house with a car, a red Escort, outside. Steve thinks I've lost it and is making all kinds of noise and trouble. I got the policeman to take off his walkie-talkie, a big mistake, and leave it at the front of the house. I've got a gun behind the policeman's back. We knock on the door and then hear an Irish voice ask who it is. The policeman says it's the police. The door's undone and there's me with the gun in his back. The policeman asked if he had a car and the Irishman said that he had, it was the red Escort. I told him to get the keys. The Irishman asked why we needed the keys. I said to him, 'Because we fucking need the keys.' With that he said, 'All right, all right.' He got the message.

As he went for the keys, a woman came down to the bottom of the stairs and looked at me standing there, but I had one gun behind my back and one gun behind the cozzer's back so she could not see any weapons. Suddenly, the Irishman's back and gives the car keys to the cozzer who, not thinking, automatically hands them to me. I can't take the keys because I've got two guns in my hands. Two .38s. The Irishman's eyes lit up and I said to him, 'And you.' I motioned him towards his car. My mind was a whirl and I didn't realise when I took the Irishman hostage that he only had his underpants on. And a vest. It didn't register with me that he was half-naked. I said to the woman, 'Don't call the police, I've got the old man, everything is going to be all right, just don't ring the police.'

We got in his car. There's the Irishman, the policeman, Steve and me. I was in the front with the policeman driving. We used the back roads through Collier Road and into Chigwell and everything seemed quite safe, when suddenly there was a police car behind us. Someone has got on to us. There were helicopters buzzing about. I told the cozzer to stop the car. I've jumped out and fired one shot, not at the police car but over the top of it. The police car disappeared. Every police car I shot at disappeared. Didn't want to know. I jumped back in the car and told him to turn around and we're driving down the road and then another police car, another police car, another police car, another police car was behind us.

By now we were doing 80mph and sometimes coasting nearer 100mph. I was concerned about where we were and asked Steve. Steve kept saying, 'Vic, I'm going to die. Vic, I'm going to die.' I kept telling him to shut up and not call me by my name. Now, he doesn't want to talk to me any more. He was using his hands, left, right, left. We get to this turning and he used his hand and I said, 'Right.' We skidded as we were going so fast and we smashed into this bridge and it seemed that the car was fucked. Later, the cozzer said he did it on purpose, but he didn't. He skidded, he was going too fast and that's what happened as we got to a place called Abridge near Epping Forest.

I jumped out, looking to see where the police cars were. I wasn't interested in the hostages, I just wanted to get Steve and myself away. The cozzer and the Irishman hopped it and I was happy to see them go – something less to worry about. I looked at these police cars. One was about 50 feet away and I started running towards it. The cozzer must have seen me with the two guns. He turned his lights off and started reversing.

I ran as fast as I could and I couldn't get to him. I turned round and I was walking down, and there was a Chinese restaurant. There were all these chinkies in there. I ran up and told one of them to give me his car keys. He had a white Capri. He was the restaurant owner, Lam Quang Tran. I got him in the back of the car and his bird wanted to get in with him. She was hysterical. I didn't want to take a bird hostage. It's a horrible thing. I pushed her away. She was screaming on the pavement, screaming and screaming.

Anyway, right now we're away. All of a sudden we're driving down the road now and police are picking up on us again but they're far behind. I had my gun on the Chinaman all the time – he was so frightened he might have done something really stupid. We got some warning shots off at the police cars. It was like one of those screeching episodes out of *The Sweeney* on telly.

The car was roaring along when Steve said, 'Stop the car, stop the car.' There was no warning. He didn't tip us that there was a house coming up that he knew. He just begged for the car to be stopped. I got the car stopped and he got out. He was more with it, and he ran into a house. I looked over my shoulder and there were all these police cars coming and if I had followed him into the house we were fucked. The cozzers would have known where we'd gone to. All of a sudden there was just me and the Chink. I looked at the Chink and said, 'Go.'

We went. Steve went in a safe house. After about ten minutes I kept opening the door so they didn't know where he got out. I covered his arse for him and made sure no one ever knew where he was. By that time, it was too late for me. I had ten police cars, armed response units, everything. All up my arse.

I knew it was only a matter of time before they tried to stop the car and shoot me dead.

I was heavily outnumbered. I decided I would make for the trees. I left the Chinese man and I was away heading through a field. I kept looking back and I saw cars pull up and teams wearing white shirts with blue vests, all the armed response units were after me.

I shot and they all ran back. I shot over their heads, not at them. I was still trying to escape, to avoid some OK Corral shoot-out.

There were countless police cars coming and I was trapped in and around the field. As I was running, I slipped over and I dug a big hole and ripped up plants and stuff and just lay there with bracken over me. I buried myself alive.

Believe it or not, that's what saved my life: running into those fields. I'd have been a dead doughnut in a shoot-out with the cozzers. No matter how many I had shot down, they would have got me in the end just by force of numbers. When the cozzers ran out, they left their footprints behind so the tracker dogs and the other police weren't sure whose footprints were which. When they found my footprints, they just ended with me in the ground. I waited another hour or two and suddenly I could hear my hunters, the voices of the police. Imagine it. I was soaking wet. I was smothered in mud. No one could see me. I was as deep in the earth as I could get. All these plants all over my head, on my body. It was a potato field with no trees, just little plants. All you could see was my left eye.

I had the guns and I thought that, if I was going to die, I was going to die properly. I had a gun in each hand. And I just lay there. When I heard these voices, I thought, 'Oh, here we go.'

It was pissing with rain. They had followed my footprints. The next minute I heard a dog sniffing away and I was thinking that at any moment it was going to come over and fucking jump on me. What I didn't know was that all the mess of mud and rain blocked the dog's senses. The dog was sniffing near me but it couldn't smell me. With that, the cozzer came to the end of the footprints and there was me in the earth. He stood on the side of my leg. One of my guns was right under his bollocks. I could have shot him straight in the nuts.

Then, they just fucked off. I thought I'd got my life back. I couldn't believe it. I lay there and they went through it two or three times and they still couldn't find me in that field. I was there for eight hours.

Much later, I looked out and there was no one about. It was sunny now. My leg was visible, the cozzer had exposed it when he stood on and next to me. I got out of the hole and crawled towards these tall weeds and plants, which were about 150 yards away. I crawled into a pig farm – and that's where all the pigs were. The uniformed ones.

It was their search headquarters. I could see them using binoculars and talking on radios. There were helicopters in the air. It was a proper manhunt. I rolled over and I saw all this commotion and I thought they'd seen me through the binoculars. I wondered whether to stand up and fight against all them with one gun. I'd got rid of the other gun. I don't want to say where. In all that tear-up I'd got rid of that other gun.

It saved my life that hidden gun. The gun I'd got wasn't the gun that shot David.

I wasn't going anywhere. The game was up.

I stood up, my arm was killing me where I'd been lying on it for eight and a half hours, and when they told me to put my hands up I couldn't. I got one arm up. The cozzers were lined up just like in the movie *Zulu*. One rank of cozzers and then another. All guns pointed at me. If they'd sprayed their bullets all over me I'd have looked like a Tetley tea bag. They had all their guns pointed at me from 30 or 40 yards away and they told me to lie down. I did. They came and handcuffed me behind my back.

They took me to the side of this van. All these armed response vans were there. They were like kids. The fox had caught the rabbit. Everyone was very pleased with themselves. They'd thought they had lost me. You could see it in their faces. By the luck of the gods they had caught me. One mistake. If I'd stayed in the ground, stayed put! One of the cozzers said to me, 'If you'd remained in that hole another hour and a half, Vic, you'd have been a free man.'

It was that dog Steve who was the free man. He'd fucked up the job and then just looked after himself, got out of trouble and left me in it. I should have blasted him at the Penthouse and walked away from it all. I've been questioned about it ever since – and the leader of the inquisition has been me. But I know deep down that I could not have lived with myself if I'd left him.

The cozzers put me in their secure van and I had to start thinking. It was lucky I knew how to work the police.

'Is that the gun you had all night?' they asked me.

'Yeah,' I said.

'Are there bullets in the gun?'

'Yeah' I said, and I set them up.

They shot themselves in the foot by verballing me up to say that that gun was the one I used to shoot everybody. It would turn out that wasn't the gun that shot David. The shooting of David was an accident, it wasn't intentional. There was no way I intended to shoot anybody or anything like that, it was a total accident that happened. It was because he grabbed the revolver. It was his fault.

They put me on an ID parade for another few robberies and I got picked out a couple of times. The cozzers got on the good cop, bad cop routine. One was giving all the heavy number, and I thought I would settle these bastards up. I told him the opposite of what had happened and they said they were going to verbal me up. I told them to do what they were going to do.

I knew I was going down – it was just a question of how long for. I had to work on my version of events. At that point it looked like David was bleeding to death. And other evidence was being gathered. It's interesting now, all these years later, to read over how the others involved saw the action. The married cozzer, PC Coult, who I kidnapped – he'd be nearly 40 years old now, in 2003 – gave a pretty detailed account of the night's events, as he saw them:

On Sunday, 25 September 1988 at approximately 3.30am I was on duty at Chadwell Heath Police Station. When, due to information received via the personal radio, I went to Ilford in a marked police Panda serial number 66013. I turned from the High Road Ilford into Hainault Street, and I had slowed down to turn left into Havelock Street when I saw a man on the footway approx. Two feet from the vehicle stood on the corner.

The man shouted and I saw in his hand a revolver handgun. He was stood with both hands on the gun. I would describe this man as white with fair hair, straight and cut short which was parted. He was clean-shaven, was stocky built between 5 foot 11 inches and 6 foot tall, and I would say in his early twenties. He appeared to have a wide mouth and *large teeth with light-coloured eyes. He spoke with a London accent. I will refer to this man as 'A'. He shouted, 'Stop the car,' and ran round the front of the Panda. He held the gun pointed at me. He said, 'Get out,' and then he called to another man who I had not seen. He was leaning against the wall. He said, 'Get in' and the man who I will now call 'B' got in the back of the Panda. I would describe him as dark-skinned, probably Mediterranean in appearance with dark curly hair like a Greek or similar. He was approx 5 foot 11 inches, stocky muscular build in his early twenties with a long face and dark eyes. As he got in the Panda 'B' said, 'I'm shot. I'm shot,' and 'A' said, 'I know.' 'A' then told me to get back in the Panda and he ran round the front of the vehicle again keeping the gun pointed at me and he got in the passenger seat.*

'A' said, 'I've shot one man tonight so drive.' He reached his right arm round the back of my seat and I felt the gun in the back of my neck. I drove up Hainault Street and into Ley Street. The man 'A' was highly excited and was shouting all the time. He was shouting, 'Go faster. Go faster,' as we drove up Ley Street.

I could hear information coming over the personal radio and I reached up to turn it down. 'A' saw me and pulled the radio off of my shirt.

We drove up Ley Street and 'A' said, 'When I tell

you to turn right, turn right.' We got to Wards Road and he said, 'Turn right.' I had seen in my mirror the R/T car J4 following at a distance and when we had turned into Wards Road it was obvious that 'A' had seen it as well, and he was trying to lose it.

I was driving with my foot to the floor and every time I took my foot off the accelerator 'A' shouted, 'Go faster. Go faster.'

We turned right to Aldborough Road South and 'A' shouted, 'Take a left. Take a left,' and I said, 'There ain't any.' He said, 'OK, go to the bottom.' When we got to the bottom, I turned left into Benton Road, and as we turned the corner, the pistol went off.

There was a big bang and I lost hearing in my left ear and the driver's window started to fall out. 'A' said, 'Sorry. I didn't mean to do that.'

We continued to drive up Cameron Road. 'A' gave a gun to 'B' in the back of the car and said, 'Cover him.' 'A' then reloaded a gun that he still had in his hand. We got to the mini roundabout at the top of Cameron Road junction with the High Road and 'A' said, 'Turn left.' We went down the High Road towards Chadwell Heath and 'A' said, 'Turn left,' and I turned into the 3rd or 4th on the left. At the top we turned right into Meads Lane and then we drove along the back streets. I could see the lights of J4 in the mirror.

'A' started screaming and shouting. He said, 'Your mates are after us, you're telling them where we are.' I said, 'I can't, you've got the radio.' He gave me the transmitter and said, 'Get rid of them,' and raised the pistol. I then called up and asked for all units to back off. By this time, we were travelling down a side road towards the High Road, Seven Kings. He then took the radio back from me again. 'A' kept shouting, 'Go faster. Go faster.' I said, 'I can't. I'll lose it and we won't be going anywhere.'

The man 'B' was lying against the side of the Panda all this time and said nothing. We turned into the High Road again he was too late. I locked the Panda up and we stopped just past the junction. He ('A') said, 'Back up.' We turned into the junction and we drove down several little roads, all of which were dead ends. He told me to drive into one of the dead ends and he suddenly was very calm. He told me to get out of the Panda. He got out and pointed the gun at me across the roof. He did not say anything.

I thought he was going to shoot me. I said, 'Is your mate all right?' He suddenly became very excited again, and said, 'Help him out.' As I took hold of the man, 'B', he said, 'Mind the ...' and stopped. When I took hold of him I could feel that his arm was all wet and I saw in the streetlights it was all blood. This is where I got the blood on my shirt. 'A' held the gun pointed towards me and we started to run. We went into a front garden, number 4, I think, and 'A' rang the doorbell and then he said to me, 'Take that off, lie down,' and tried to rip my radio off. He shouted, 'Take it off, take it off.' So I did and left it in the garden. The light came on in the house and 'A' held the gun in both hands and pointed it at me. He said, 'Tell him you're Old Bill and get his keys.' The man opened the door and 'A' held the gun above my shoulder. I said to the occupier, who I will call 'C', 'Have you got keys?' He said, 'Why?' I said, 'Have you got keys?' He said, 'Yes.' We all went into the house: myself, Suspect 'A' and the occupier. Suspect 'A' was highly excited. He was shouting, 'Come on, come on.' I said to the occupier 'C', 'What car have you got?' He said, 'A red Escort.' We all went back through the house and I saw a woman on the stairs in a black dressing-gown. We all walked out to the front gate and 'A' ran back in. He pointed the gun at the woman and said, 'If you call the Old Bill, I've got your old man.' He ran back out. He was shouting, 'Where's the car? Where's the car?' We went to a red D reg Escort and I unlocked the door and stood back. The man 'A' pointed the gun at me and said, 'Get in and drive.' I got in and civilian Mr 'C' got in the passenger seat, the suspect 'B' got in and 'A' was still outside. I said to 'B', 'Talk to your *mate, you need help.' He didn't say anything. 'A' then got in behind me.*

He screamed, 'Drive.' I said, 'I don't know Romford.' He said, 'Drive.' We went through Collier Row and ended up on the dual carriageway towards Chigwell.

Whilst we were driving along the road 'A' wound down the window, put the pistol out of the window and pulled the trigger. There was a click and he brought the gun back in. We got to the lights at the end of the road and there was a pub on the right-hand side. I think we went straight over and down a country lane and through Abridge. As we came into Abridge, I saw one Essex Panda parked on the right-hand side. We continued through Abridge and we were travelling at 95 miles per hour and I saw the lights of the Panda come on behind me and I knew the suspect 'A' would realise it was a police car so I tried to keep in front of the lights but he saw them and he started screaming, 'It's a cop car, lose it, lose it, faster.'

The civilian in the front was murmuring, 'Too fast, too fast.' I told him to shut up and then 'A' said to him, 'Get on the floor,' and he didn't react so 'A' screamed at him, 'Get down.' I reached over and pushed him down. We came to a roundabout and 'A' said, 'Go left.' We were travelling too fast and I locked the car up. We went straight after the roundabout. 'A' said, 'Keep it going,' and poked me with the gun. I managed to get it on to the road signposted for Ongar and 'A' said, 'When I tell you to stop, stop.'

We went under a large bridge for the motorway and he said, 'Stop.' I heard the Essex Panda coming up behind us and then the engine note changed. 'A' had got out of the back of the car and as the Essex Police car passed us he followed it with his gun and shot at it once. He got back in and was screaming hysterically, 'Turn round here.' As I was trying to find the reverse etc., he was shouting, 'Come on, come on.' We went back to the roundabout. I went the wrong side of it and back on the road to Abridge. We were still travelling at high speed, between 80 and 90mph all the time. 'A' was shouting, 'Faster, faster' again. I told him I would lose it if we went faster. I said to 'A', 'This bloke is getting on my nerves. We don't need him,' meaning the civilian. He said, 'Find a dark road, we'll lose this bloke.'

He then said to the civilian something about 'I know where you live so don't say anything.' I was looking for somewhere, when the lights for the Panda reappeared. 'A' said, 'Fuck it, we'll keep him.'

'A' saw the lights and he said to me, 'I've shot one bloke tonight, I'm not afraid to shoot you if I'm going out in a blaze of glory.'

I said, 'Don't hurt me.' He said, 'All right mate,

just keep driving.' We then came back into Abridge and I had had enough. I decided we were not going any further. 'A' said 'Turn right.'.

I picked the biggest bit of kerb I could find and aimed for it. I hit the kerb and said, 'The steering's gone,' but it hadn't. 'A' said, 'Go and wake that bloke up.' I got out of the car and waited until the suspects had run around the corner. I said to the passenger get out and find some place to hide. I watched while he hid behind some cars across the road in a garage. When I was sure that they hadn't seen where I'd gone, I went back past the car and the Essex Panda drove past. I think suspect 'A' raised his pistol but I don't think he fired. I then jumped over the wall of the bridge. I heard one of the suspects shout, 'There's a Capri here.' I fell down a bank and walked along the river until I saw the Essex R/T car …

In this country there's not many people who've had gun battles with the police. The cozzers didn't say they were running after me. All the other police said they hid behind the cars. The cozzers don't mind shooting at someone but when that someone's shooting back at them it's a different matter. They don't like that and that's when the machine guns and all the posing comes out.

When it comes to it, they're all out there and ready to spray you up and down with bullets. Now, I think, if it came to it and I fancied my chances and maybe even if I didn't, I'd pick up the gun and have a go. I'd rather go that way and end up dead. I certainly could easily have been dead after the Penthouse. As David nearly was.

By the time they had me in custody that was my priority – David's condition. I was very concerned about him for my life was riding on his. I had every reason to be. They used 48 pints of blood to help keep him alive.

CHAPTER NINE

BREAKOUT

'I'VE DONE MORE PORRIDGE THAN
THE THREE BEARS.'

**VICTOR DARK TO JUDGE IAN GRAEME MCLEAN
AT THE OLD BAILEY, 3 JANUARY 1990**

As the charges against me were being gathered – and there were plenty, so it was taking time – I learned more about the aftermath of my raid on the Penthouse. David had been rushed to the King George Hospital in Newbury Park, Ilford. They showed me the notes of Dr Jay Pandya who worked with the geezer who operated on David. He described the injuries to David better than I ever could:

> He [David] had sustained several gunshot wounds. He had been shot through the left side of the lower abdomen, the right hand and the left upper arm. He was apparently resuscitated in the ambulance and further resuscitation was carried out in the Casualty Department by Casualty Officers.

My assessment of his wounds was limited by the fact that there was an urgency to resuscitate the individual, and to prepare him for immediate surgery.

Injuries consisted of: Left arm: 1cm hole over upper outer aspect of the arm laterally, left arm, 1cm hole over upper aspect of the arm medially. Right hand: ragged hole with burns around it with palm lacerations. Abdominally: a superficial graze in the left hypochondrial region measuring approximately 1cm x 5cm in diameter and a 1cm laceration and haematoma in the region of the left groin. His femoral pulses were palpable, the right being more palpable than the left. Both pedal pulses on the right and left were palpable, but again, the right were greater than the left. Upon completion of resuscitation he was swiftly taken to theatre.

He was operated upon his hand and arm by Mr Chen, the Orthopaedic Consultant and abdominally by Mr Pearson, Consultant Surgeon. It was revealed that the bullet had taken away the front of the main artery to the left leg, and had become embedded in the left hipbone. A new artificial artery was stitched in to replace the damaged femoral artery, and this restored good circulation to the left leg.

Post-operatively he was taken to the Intensive Care Unit but he continued to bleed and, in fact, in total required some 48 pints of blood. He was swiftly rushed back to the operating theatre in the afternoon of the day of admission, and his abdomen was re-explored, and more blood was evacuated from it, though no actual bleeding point was found. However, at the same time a bleeding point in the left upper arm was secured by Mr Chen.

His post-operative recovery was somewhat stormy, but he has continued to make very good recovery. There has been some evidence of nerve damage supplying the skin of the left inner side of the left knee and thigh. Laceration to his right hand has limited the movement of his hand, but in due course things will improve.

He has been extremely lucky to have survived such a vicious attack.

There you have it, the nuts and bolts of David's injuries. The consultant surgeon, J B Pearson, didn't help my situation by declaring of David: 'Needless to say, after such a murderous attack, he is extremely lucky to have survived.'

And I wanted to survive too. I didn't fancy my chances in court. Would you after such an evening out?

I'd appeared at Redbridge Magistrates Court accused of attempting to murder David. I also had five further charges, of causing grievous bodily harm to David, robbery with intent, possession of a firearm while committing an indictable offence, possession of a firearm with intent to resist arrest and threatening to kill a police officer. They remanded me in custody for three days while the law took its due process. I took mine too.

I tried my first breakout five days after the Penthouse raid. It was early afternoon on 30 September 1988, and I was being taken the short trip from Hackney police station to Wormwood Scrubs Prison in London. There was a sergeant and a police constable in charge of the Ford Transit van. It had a screened-off driver's cab, a double-bolted side door and bars on the windows. I played the nice quiet lad. I was all sweetness and light – on the outside.

Inside, I was seething and plotting. I wanted away. We were driving along Gray's Inn Road towards Euston Road and I knew the driver was watching me. He had adjusted his mirror so he could get full sights on me. These two hadn't taken any chances. They had put one set of handcuffs on my right wrist, another set on the window bars and then joined them together. The daisy chain meant I was handcuffed to the van.

I thought, 'Fuck it.' They never expected me to try anything. Who could get out of this security van?

I decided to Rambo it. I tore the window grille away from the bodywork of the van and with that the bars came away, and although the handcuffs were still on my right wrist they were free of the van. I kicked the window out of the nearside. I was clambering out of the window space when the sergeant appeared and grabbed for my leg. I pulled back. The other cozzer came round the back of the van just as I put my head and shoulders out – ready to squeeze my way through. He grabbed at me and got me but I was determined to make it, so I kept struggling, fighting my way out. These two cozzers were screaming like girls. They were squealing, 'Help, help' and by then there were lots of people around.

But I wasn't giving up. The cozzer had a good hold on me though and was stopping me getting out the window. The other one was on the radio calling for more Old Bill. Then he was back and as I heard sirens in the distance the two of them managed to cuff me again to the van.

I'd ripped the side of the van off. If only I had got me feet on the ground …

Teams of cozzers arrived and I was trussed up, handcuffed and packed into the van. I had four cozzers inside the van with me – and the two up front. They were not a happy bunch. They stared at me all the way. They couldn't believe someone was strong enough to tear up the side of their precious Transit. They took me off to Holborn nick and chucked me, handcuffed, into a cell. I finally got to the Scrubs but I suppose you could say we took the long way round.

I was on remand for a long time, about 18 months in all. In London's Brixton Prison. I was a 'Cat AA', a top-security boy, but I had all the perks of a remanded prisoner. It is best to allow remand to go on as long as you can because you get a visit every day and the time goes against any sentence. You can eat as much as you want and the food is not the swill – and the tampered stuff – you get when you are doing time proper. You do yourself a favour staying on remand.

But I didn't want any of that. I wanted my freedom. I didn't want any more of Brixton than I had already experienced.

I had another breakout planned. It was typical of me to try and escape from Brixton, to try and make it out of 'D seg', the massively caged part of the jail segregated off for the real bad boys. It's the most secure unit in Great Britain. Well, if you're going to have a go …

A set of mates of mine, a neat little team on the outside, were in on the escape. It was nothing sophisticated – a simple plan to go over the wall. 'D seg' at Brixton is a special building with cages all around it. It's a prison within a prison.

The unit held a dozen of us – rated the most dangerous men in Britain.

Most of them were IRA and were Irish, not some foreigners who were working for them. I was one of four Englishmen. The security was strict and everywhere you moved there were watchers, guards with dogs. In Brixton, they were very serious about keeping us locked up.

I figured the only way to escape was to get religion, to put myself in the hands of God. The church was the way out. At least, one specific place of worship. Going to church in Brixton was always complex, an elaborate procedure, through three sets of automatic doors. After the first door, there is a 'sterile' area where you are thoroughly searched, and then you go through the other sets of doors and into the church.

As I was an 'A' man I was taken to church surrounded by four screws and a couple of dog handlers. I could feel their eyes on me all the time. I did dry runs at the church for a couple of weeks. The plan was to get away from the screws and make it to the wall. Flares would go up from the outside to pinpoint the spot where there would be two aluminium ladders and a lorry, courtesy of an East End borough council – I won't say which one – waiting for me. The ladders would be chained together and one would come my side of the wall. I was going to scarper, up and over, down the ladder and off in the lorry.

The timing was going to be co-ordinated by radio. A radio 'bug' was smuggled into the nick for me. Outside an old guy was going be walking his dog and listening to a Walkman. I'd alert him when I was outside the church. The green light, the 'Go!', would happen when the flare went off.

One great snag – the 'bug' had two frequencies. I could be heard on one, but not the other. All the radio traffic was incoming, so they could not hear that I was on my way. But I was.

I went out from the church, the prison guards were

there, but I turned and trimmed one. I punched him out, his feet went in the air and he was knocked out. With that, I was off. I ran about 100 yards and then I took a right and ran another 100 yards. I took a left behind Brixton's reception. I thought the signal had gone but there was no flare. I thought to myself that they were definitely going to be there. They wouldn't let me down these people because I'd worked with them on many things.

The reception area had no gate so I could get between the fence and the prison wall. I did another sprint, another 100 yards in seconds. I stopped at the wall and shouted, 'John! John!' He hadn't got the signal but he heard me and he fired the flare.

The flare hit the outside wall, smoke billowed up and then, with a flash and a bang, the other flare came over on the prison side of the wall. I thought I was in the middle of *The Great Escape*. I stopped for a moment, just getting the feel of it all. I turned around – there's an Alsatian running right for me. I can see its mad eyes – and the teeth.

Now I was running too. I wrapped my jacket around my arm and stopped, turned and faced down the dog. It went smack into my arm and grabbed me in its jaws. I kicked the dog in the throat and it was out of it.

I was shouting, 'John! John!' but the timing was way out and they thought it had all gone high hookey and shot off.

I was there, between the wall and the fence. There were about 30 screws on one side, the same number on the other.

I was piggy in the middle. They were furious and ordered me to lie down. Some officer ordered a search. At the same time all the cons are shouting from the prison windows, 'Let him alone! Let him alone!' They were loving it.

I looked around and, well, I was going to get a good beating anyhow so I just ran straight into them. I got a few of them, an elbow there, a fist there, a knee there. But that was that.

I got battered. They just smashed me to pieces. The fists and boots went into me. I was trying to escape. I was resisting capture. They didn't need any excuses after that. It was thump and thump, kick and kick. I knew how to protect my crucial bits but I was a bloodied mess by the end of it. They put me into another segregation unit. The Governor knew there had been a firm outside to get me out. He pulled me out of segregation and put me back in D seg and locked me up in a cage for six months. He dealt with my escape attempt within the prison system. They weren't sure how sophisticated the gang outside had been. It could have turned out to be really embarrassing for them.

It was a lot more than embarrassing for me. By January 1990, I was standing in the dock at the Old Bailey. Peering down at me from the bench was His Honour, Judge Ian Graeme McLean, a Scotsman who did not have a great sense of humour. Especially when he heard the charges against me. I could hear his disdain for me in his precise Edinburgh tones.

Steve had vanished and I stood alone in court with the weight of all that had happened during and after the Penthouse raid on me. I had time to think again about what a mug I had been. I could have put a bullet through his head and walked away. People still wonder why I didn't. But as I stood there at the Bailey I knew there was nothing I could do about the past. I had to move on, deal with what was happening in the present.

The law did not have the gun with which David was hurt. But they had plenty of witnesses, including the hostages and especially the copper PC Coult. I was in the frame and there was no real way around it for me. Except mitigation, working to reduce the heavy sentence I knew would be handed out by a judge who gave his recreation in *Who's Who* as 'gardening'. Shit, he was certainly going to plant me.

I admitted assaulting David, who had recovered well, using a firearm to resist arrest and with intent to endanger life, three charges of kidnapping and trying to escape from a police van.

I said that I had been forced to take part in the Penthouse raid by Steve, who was an East End gang leader! I refused to name this big-time gangster who I said I owed big money to. I remember telling the court: 'He's an Arthur Daley but a bit more serious. I got caught up in something that seemed right out of a *Rambo* movie.' I know the story did me some good but not how much. And I told the judge: 'I've done more porridge than the three bears.'

Judge McLean certainly did not have a sense of humour about that. He warned: 'Only a very long sentence of imprisonment will stop this sort of thing.' And this was the line-up:

1 *Assault with intent to rob: 5 years.*
2 *Possession of a firearm with intent to rob: 3 years.*
3 *Using a firearm to resist arrest: 7 years.*
4 *Assault with intent to resist arrest: 2 years.*
5 *Kidnapping: 7 years.*
6 *Kidnapping: 7 years.*
7 *Kidnapping: 7 years.*
8 *Attempt/using a firearm to resist arrest: 1 year.*

That lot added up to a nice 39 years in jail!

But with some of the sentences to run concurrent it came down to 24 years in jail. It was still a lifetime, no matter how much I juggled the arithmetic. I could have put a bullet through my mate's head and walked away. Today I think I should have. I did a long time for that slag. But in the moment my code of honour won and if I was shooting my way out he was going with me. They said it would have been easier on me if I'd grassed him up but that was never an option.

When the judge told me: 'You're going to prison for 24 years,' I just went: 'Fuck you!' They'd all expected me to break down in the box and I was glad I was able to come up with that bravado. It made me feel better to give the judge and the system the big finger. Not happy, but warmer inside myself.

For I knew how heavy the judge was going to be. His wig was rapping away, he was in a real lather. He had the hump with me. I was ready to kick off, really ready to blow off again, but then there was some hope.

Judge McLean banged on that it was only 'good fortune' that someone hadn't got killed – or more people shot – in the Penthouse raid and all that bloody bollocks afterwards. Nevertheless, because I'd coughed to the charges, he was going to set the length of the actual sentence at 18 years. It was better, but …

And as I walked down the stairs to the holding cells a screw said to me, 'That outburst didn't do your career any good.' I just went: 'Ah fuck off, you prick!' For me, at that moment, that was it. But, of course, it wasn't.

When I got that 18 years, I lay in my cell and looked at the walls and thought, 'How the fuck am I going to get through this?' I knew that they had me down as a subversive and I knew I'd do a lot down the blocks.

The lawyers went to work and, finally, the sentence was cut by three years. In the end I got 15 years for all that and, as results go, it was a reasonable one. I served ten years and two weeks for that fucked-up night. If I'd blasted that Steve off the face of the earth, it would all have been different.

But then I wouldn't have my daughter Megan. She's a 'Cat AA' baby – only one of four in the country.

We were the most feared men in the prison system but to keep us happy they would let us have visits where we could have sex. It was never acknowledged but it went on. It would never happen in the 21st century. But it went and four of us can prove it with our kids. My Megan will be ten years old in 2003. A 'Cat AA' girl: a little bit extra special.

CHAPTER TEN

CAT IN A
HOT CELL

'THE SMILEY BADGE WAS A CODE FOR SEX, IT
MEANT YOU COULD HAVE IT AWAY ON A VISIT.'

**VICTOR DARK EXPLAINING HOW HIS DAUGHTER WAS
CONCEIVED WHILE HE WAS A HIGH-SECURITY GUEST OF
HER MAJESTY'S PRISON SERVICE**

As I predicted, I was all around the blocks, all around the penal system, in this prison and then the next. I have to say that Whitemoor in Cambridgeshire was the most fun. It was the only place where the sort of sex I wanted was available: regular.

I was locked in Parkhurst on the Isle of Wight for the Penthouse balls-up, a convicted high-risk prisoner. Yet legally I was entitled to visits. Because Parkhurst was so far away from my family, they set my visits at Whitemoor – only 45 minutes away for my mum and for Carole.

My domestic set-up has changed now, but I had been with Carole for some time. She's the mother of my teenage son Luke – and Megan who my mother never believed would be conceived. She didn't know the law!

I got my legal entitlement of time at Whitemoor for the visits and it extended to three months. Paradise!

I wanted to get to Whitemoor because it is close to home but then I learned you could have sex on visits. That made Whitemoor a priority. The smiley badge was the code – that little face with a grin in the middle of it. In Parkhurst, we'd get letters from the geezers down at Whitemoor, other prison inmates. They couldn't be blatant about it but they'd say the visits were very good or fantastic, and there would be the smiley badge.

That little face with a smile – I'll never forget it. I heard through people coming back to Parkhurst about what was happening. Only high-risk prisons could do it. They were physically locking you in rooms on your own with your visitor. I was told time in Whitemoor was set and shortly afterwards my mum and her mate Lil came to see me at Parkhurst. I told her that Carole and I were going to have another baby. My mum and Lil started laughing. I asked her what the joke was. 'You can't have a baby in prison,' she said. I said I would, she should wait and see. They just laughed at me, thought I'd cracked up, I suppose. No chance of that with what I had on the horizon. And on my mind.

Four or five visits a week, about two and a half hours duration every time.

A couple of my family used to bring Carole over to see me. The procedure was strict as we were 'Cat AA' prisoners but there were no television cameras. They didn't want visitors smuggling stuff in, drugs and the like, so there was a clothing rule. You went in one set of clothes, changed into a 'sterile' set and then went into the visit and vice versa. The screws kept the set worn during the visit and checked it out.

But I wasn't thinking about smuggling. For about 12 weeks, I was involved in nothing but sex.

Carole wore a long dress and we were discreet – at first. She used to sit on my lap and her dress would hang over, disguising the action. If the screw had walked in – and they never did – all they would have seen was her sitting in my lap with a long dress on. We were in the room on our own all the time.

The first week, she was obviously a bit frightened, a bit cautious, but after that we thought, so to speak, we'd got a fucking licence. We were down the end of the landing, the door was shut and nobody bothered us. The prison guards were reading the paper or playing dominoes. If they wanted you they'd knock on the door and shout, 'You've got ten minutes.' That would be the end of the visit.

They knew what was going on. Towards the end, people were starting to be very blatant with it and that's why they stopped it. They knocked down all the closed-off visiting units and just made it one big open one and introduced closed-circuit television cameras. I don't suppose you can get a kiss now. Just a kiss-off.

There were some problems with some screws – probably faggots. We wore our own stuff – not prison uniforms then. Some of the screws liked to watch the show when you undressed. The procedure was that you had a box for the clothes you took off and one for the new gear. The screws were not allowed to have you stripped naked. You would take your T-shirt off and, when you'd put your T-shirt back on, then you'd pull your shorts down and flick 'em and then pull them back up. It was all done for decency.

Unless they wanted to be funny and wanted you to take your shorts off. If you had a short T-shirt, you were in trouble because all your knackers were hanging out. But you got horrible bastards like one I had at an arrival point.

He said to me, 'Lift your top up.'

I said, 'Are you a poof or something?'

He said, 'Everyone does it – you'll be down the block if you don't.'

I said to him, 'You'll have to take me down the block for you're breaking all the laws. You're not allowed to do that.'

He didn't know what to do.

I said to him: 'I've been in prison 19 years – don't talk to me about strip searching.' He and his mate were just a pair of faggots. I used the robes that we were entitled to wear between changes of clothes. It was worth the hassle.

The proof of that is Megan was conceived in HM Prison Whitemoor. As I said, there are only four of these girls in the country. And they were all girls. It was a standing joke, like it must have been something in the water. I believe it was something to do with the romance of it all!

She's a special kid and she doesn't even know it yet. I've never told her how unique she is. She doesn't know where she was conceived. She hasn't even asked those questions. She's a special baby in special circumstances which if you told someone, they might find hard to believe. Any doubters – I'll take a blood test and prove scientifically that she's my child. Anyway, she's got my good nature. And that should be proof enough for sensible geezers.

I've done things that people can only fucking dream of.

Yet, locked-up life is not all sex and home brew. As I've told you, the British penal system is more Charles Dickens than Barbara Cartland. Whatever the conditions, every prisoner has time to reflect. I certainly did. Most of all I thought I was lucky over the Penthouse raid. David survived for one – and the judge knew I could have killed lots of cozzers that night if I had wanted to. The cozzers are so used to shooting people that aren't shooting back that they stay down and out of trouble when gunfights happen.

Armed police aren't that brave when they are ducked down behind a car or, more likely, an armoured van. That night I saw lots of white shirts wearing flak jackets coming for me and I fired over their heads. There was lots of boom, boom action but I never aimed at a target, I was shooting in the sky.

That Judge McLean at the Old Bailey knew, fucking

knew, that I could have killed loads of the cozzers. When the cozzer I took hostage said my gun went off behind his head the judge asked me: 'Did you mean to shoot the policeman?'

I said, 'Look, if I want to kill a policeman I could have killed loads of them that night. Loads of them.'

And he knew it from the evidence. And I knew every word of evidence, for in prison you go over it again and again, go over the paperwork and the pictures of what really happened in your head. I knew the police could have done nothing if I had wanted to kill a score or more of them. There was nothing they could have done. Most of them acted like screaming girls.

But on a robbery, as I said, I didn't go out with the intention to hurt people, not on a robbery. I'm not a nasty person.

Obviously I've hurt a lot of people. But they were people who I knew had to be done, because they were going to hurt me. Or they were going to hurt a friend of mine. That's where my problems have been in life. I avoided confrontations but when one came along I dealt with it. I had to. It was part of me. I could not walk away.

Many people offered me work, lots of it, years ago, asking if I could do this, if I could do that to people. I said no. I explained that you could get 20 large from an armed robbery – but you didn't get paid twenty large to take someone off the planet.

I looked at the percentages. One, I don't like killing people for the sake of it and, two, I could get the same money for doing a robbery.

The only time I would have taken part in something like that in the past is if something serious had come up. A situation where no diplomacy would win – you know *they* are going to go. Or *you* are going to go.

In that sort of situation you deal with it. What's the choice?

I also had time to think, lots and lots, about how my principles cost me fucking dearly when I did have a choice. Straight people will never understand it – how I made that policeman pick up my mate and get him in the car. How many people would have made the cozzer do that? How many people would have hung around for all that nonsense? No one in Britain has done that. And I didn't have to do that for that man but because I'm steeped in principles I did.

People in my world like that. They made me out to be star. I don't want to be on that pedestal. I'm not looking for that. I'm just telling it the way it is – not to be a hero of my world. The only thing I can be a hero about is principles. I'm proud of my principles. You look in any book over the past 30 years for a man who has got his injured mate away and got a policeman to carry him and you will find zero. It had never happened before.

But that geezer never telephoned me. Never came down to visit me. I took two and a half large off him.

That's not a lot for ten years, is it? Carole got nothing from him. He knew the score more than anybody but acted like a slug about it. He never helped her out while I was away. That principle cost me ten years. Yet, if any of you lot, turning the pages of my book now, were in our gang and someone came along and attacked you, I would still pick you up and try and take you away. No matter how useless or gutless you might be. If you're part of my team, that's it. My principles haven't changed. My solicitor during the Penthouse trial turned around to me and said, 'You know what, Vic? You would have made a fucking brilliant soldier.'

Now I am a little older, I look at these geezers going into Bosnia or Iraq and I think to myself, 'They're the heroes.' If I was back in my twenties I could have been one of them. I would have loved it, the excitement of it.

It was the same with armed robbery. There's a crossover between the money and the excitement. After a successful robbery you feel there is nothing that you cannot do. Which is why I did it again and again. People knew me or knew of me and the major message they received was that I had no fear. Literally, no fucking fear. Which made me a very dangerous man.

Which is why I was in Parkhurst Prison, one of Britain's more legendary nicks, where even the little office is protected with bullet-proof glass. Parkhurst had the reputation of being one of the toughest jails and it was understandable. They had a Special Security Block (SSB) and over the years that contained masterspy George Blake and a couple of the Great Train Robbers, Charlie Wilson – who ended up getting gunned down in Spain – and poor old Ronnie Biggs.

I know a lot of Parkhurst's history because, just like straight people look up the details of the hotel where they are staying, I've always liked to know something about the nicks I've been bunged into. And Parkhurst goes all the way back to the 1700s when they decided to look after 'juvenile prisoners' – some kids only six years old – and get them off rotting sailing ships and bang 'em up proper. Can you imagine?

The prison buildings were already there and I don't think they've changed much in 400 years. The big advantage in those days of being on the Isle of Wight was the water, the anchorage where the ships could pick up the little villains and sail them off to Botany Bay. Later, they ran it as a military camp and then a women's prison but the only women when I got there were pretend ones. They had riots and some sad souls who languished in what we'd call a 'seg' unit, but they knew as a lunatic asylum.

It felt like a lunatic asylum in 1995 when three cons, Andrew Rodger, Matthew Williams and Keith Rose, two of them 'Cat As', escaped. All the screws had red faces. The lads were on the run on the island – they never got off the Isle of Wight – for seven days and it was funnier than

Ronnie Barker in *Porridge*. One of them was a qualified pilot and they planned to fly off the island, but the plane they nicked had a flat battery and they were caught. If that plane had fired up they would have been gone good and proper. It was one of the most embarrassing escapes to happen anywhere. To any prison.

It began a political witchhunt – and Parkhurst has never been the same since. They moved out all the 'Cat As' like me and downgraded the place to a 'B' prison. You don't get the high class of prisoner there now.

Parkhurst, once the port of call for George Blake, the Great Train Robbers and people like Ronnie and Reg Kray, was just left with the legend.

And it was because of Parkhurst that I became friends with Reg Kray. And helped a young man who later carried Reg's coffin.

CHAPTER ELEVEN

CODE OF HONOUR

'VIC DARK LOOKED AFTER FRIENDS OF MINE IN
THE PRISON SYSTEM. I SENT HIM A LETTER
THANKING HIM, AND AFTER THAT WE BECAME
FRIENDS. VIC WAS ALWAYS A STAUNCH MEMBER
OF THE PRISON COMMUNITY.'

REG KRAY

I was that tough little kid trying to join The Pastures youth club in Leytonstone when Reg Kray first went to Parkhurst in 1969. It was chance that was to allow me to know him better.

Banged up in Parkhurst in 1992 when I was there was Bradley Allardyce. He had been convicted of a couple of armed robberies and got a 12-year stretch. He was tall and thin and nervous. Some contacts of mine knew his family and I was asked to watch out for him. And that's what I did.

Bradley's brother Andrew killed himself while Bradley was locked up but he was allowed to attend the funeral – like a dog. He was held on a six-foot chain by his prison guard escort. The screws even had him chained when he helped carry his brother's coffin to the grave. Now Bradley was nervous before this but afterwards he was almost a basket case over his brother's death.

I talked to him a lot – I had learned my share of counselling inside – and helped him through the time. Bradley was moved out to Maidstone Prison a couple of years later, and that's where he and Reg Kray became close friends. During their talks, Bradley told Reg about my help.

Which is why Reg, who said he knew of me from my reputation, wrote and thanked me for being a friend to Bradley 'during his time of need'. After that, I suppose you would call us pen-friends. We wrote a lot of letters to each other and I understood more about the code of honour that exists in the world I used to be part of. Most importantly, that loyalty and respect are paramount.

I followed Reg's fight for freedom and I believe he was a political prisoner. No Home Secretary wanted the flak for having allowed one of the twins out from behind bars. Ron Kray, who had been locked away in Broadmoor, died there in 1995, supposedly of a heart attack. Reg was never certain about that. The twins' older brother, Charlie, went out in April 2000. By the time of Reg's funeral in October that year I was out of prison – I'd done my ten years, two months and three weeks for the Penthouse – and, considering all that had happened, had no intention of ever going inside again. I thought it was appropriate that I paid my respects at the funeral.

I was still a 'Cat A' prisoner when I was released from Frankland Prison after the Penthouse sentence. I'd served more than nine years as a double 'AA', but by the time I got out I was down to a single 'A' man. I remember the day I walked out. The screws were as normal as ever: unhelpful bastards. I asked one of them, 'Has my brother turned up yet?' He gave me a disdainful look. 'No one here for *you*, Dark.' Just then another screw ran up. 'Fucking hell, someone has just rolled up in an enormous Bentley. It's right outside the gates.'

My brother had arrived – in his £258,000 convertible Bentley, the same model Will Smith the movie star has. I must admit I swaggered out of there and into the Bentley. It was my two fingers up to them all. My brother had champagne in the car and we celebrated. I was *out*. And as I drank the champagne I swore that I was going to stay *out* – I did not want to be an old man in prison, an old man at the mercy of the system.

I understood a lot from what happened to Reg Kray. He had been given a 'minimum' sentence of 30 years, which he began in Parkhurst before, like me, being moved about the prison system. But it was only in his last hours – when he died at the Town House Hotel near Norwich – that he was 'free'. He was 66 when he died, but even after all the years locked up he regarded himself as a successful man. Certainly he had influenced a lot of people not to take his route.

I wish I had known better when I was a kid. I wouldn't recommend 'armed robber' as a career choice for any kid. Prison, as I've detailed for you, is no holiday camp whether you accept their system or you fight it.

For Reg, most of his final days might as well have been in a jail cell – he was still imprisoned. He saw the irony, made jokes about it. Instead of the bars and handcuffs which contained him for nearly half his life, he was his own captive. And he could do nothing about it. It was his own life-support system which trapped him in ten-foot by ten-foot of hospital space, smaller than any of the jail cells he inhabited for all those years of incarceration. Flickering medical monitors watched him more carefully than any screw.

The snaking tubes attached to him, fulfilling his body's life-giving functions and constant need for pain-killing medication, had him far more under control than the penal system ever did.

His fifth-floor room, overlooking a school playground, at the Norfolk and Norwich Hospital was a less carefree confinement than the jail years which he spent as an aristocrat around England's prison community. His 32 years of jail time ended at Wayland Prison in Norfolk and by then, for many of us, he was a folk hero. He wore a gold bracelet with the word 'Legend' engraved on it, and it set off his immaculate appearance. He always washed and ironed his own clothes and was fanatical about personal cleanliness.

Reg Kray was the lifer's lifer. But what kept him going was the day when he would be a free man. Fate intervened.

Although parole after parole had been denied he still hoped, but when unconditional liberty arrived at 10.47am on 26 August 2000, on orders of then British Home Secretary Jack Straw, it was on compassionate grounds. And by then, he had been moved from prison to a hospital ward for the desperately ill. As it turned out, it was modern medicine which gave Reg more time as a free man.

He had no need to worry about 'respect' from fellow inmates but the treatment of the doctors and nurses around him. It was constant and he was grateful for their every attention. And calm, always calm, in an eerily knowing way. Reg told a friend of mine: 'I found early on in the prison system that the only way to survive was to be your own man and to be true to yourself. I was a loner in some ways in the prison system but I always had my family to support me.

'Now I don't want people to think that I am talking about the Mafia family, or to misinterpret what I am saying. I am talking about close bonds with friends and family who have been loyal and honest throughout the years. I had this fantasy that freedom would mean the opening of the prison gates as though in one of those Humphrey Bogart or Jimmy Cagney movies. You know, when all the cars are there to greet you and you go off and have a big party …'

As I said, you have to be strong to survive prison and that's what is so wrong with the system. They lock some poor sod away, and he just sinks. People like Reg could survive it, but drugs – and those addicted to them – have taken over the system just as they have the streets and it is becoming a much worse place than he ever experienced. Or I have. They kill people for pennies today. When he died, Reg had his wife, Roberta, whom he married inside Maidstone Prison on 14 July 1997, with him. Also nearby were Bradley Allardyce and his wife, Donna, who he had married inside Maidstone on 24 October 1996. I hadn't seen Bradley since Parkhurst until that day of Reg's funeral: 12 October 2000, at St Matthew's Church, Bethnal Green.

I'd walked along the Bethnal Green Road and watched the end of an era in the East End. It was quite a sight, sad but also inspiring. The ceremonies began outside the premises of W. English and Son, which also looked after the funerals of Reg's brothers and mother. In the road, six black horses stood in front of the hearse; making up the cortege were 18 black limousines, weighed down by flowers from friends. On the way the procession – preceded by the head undertaker in silk top hat and floral coat – passed the church where Reg married his first wife, Frances Shea, in 1965, and it went down Vallance Road, where the twins were brought up by their beloved mother, Violet, who died in 1982. At the church there were 150 security guards in ankle-length navy overcoats, 'RKF' (Reg Kray Funeral) badges and red armbands.

Inside, the church was packed: there were almost so many people you could not tell who was there but I saw Roy Shaw and Joe Pyle and other familiar faces. There were lots of actor types and would-be gangsters but also the hard core of East Enders who know the score.

Freddie Foreman and Tony Lambrianou stayed away for reasons that are not my business. The pall-bearers were Tony Mortimer, who used to sing with East 17, and five others including Bradley. Bradley had been one of the people who spoke in church. He said in tribute, 'I look for the words, but there are none.' The service began with the tune 'Amapola', taken from the soundtrack of the Sergio Leone movie *Once Upon a Time in America*. We sang 'Morning Has Broken', 'Fight the Good Fight' and 'Abide With Me'. Most people smiled when the coffin was carried out to Sinatra singing 'My Way'. At Chingford Cemetery, Reg was buried alongside first wife, Frances, his brothers and their mother, Violet.

I found it a strange day. There were press people and television crews all over the church and at the cemetery. It was a media circus. People kept coming up to me and asking, 'What do you think about Reggie's funeral?' I said, 'Yeah, it went really well.'

Yet, I didn't feel it was the man's funeral. What haunted me that day was the injustice of it all – he was never going to get out of jail in a celebratory way. He was only released when he was dying – they'd never have let him out alive and that was wrong. Reggie killed one geezer and got 30 years. That was the sentence but he served that and more. Others who have done much worse go out long before such a stretch. It was just that in his time there weren't many people like that, whereas today the druggies are stabbing and killing geezers every minute of the day. They took him all the way to the wall and he should have been allowed out earlier.

So, that funeral day there was the sadness of his passing but also the anger at the Government for not behaving reasonably. I was pissed off and people kept asking me what I thought. It wasn't my place to say too much.

As far as I saw it, the Government killed Reg Kray. They always hated the following the twins had. God Bless Reg Kray.

Me, I got lucky on the domestic front.

CHAPTER TWELVE

REPUTATION

'I GET PHONE CALLS ALL THE TIME FROM
PEOPLE THINKING I AM AFTER THEM, PEOPLE
BEGGING ME NOT TO KILL THEM.'

VICTOR DARK, 2003

It's one of the great Hollywood clichés, the story of the gangster who gets out of prison, wants to go straight, but is drawn back into the life – usually for one last job, for a big score or to help a friend.

I'd had more than enough of helping friends. For very good reason. And I had no plans to go back to my old ways or back to jail. Lucky for me my brother is a successful businessman. He gave me a job with his company, one with a good wage. The other great bit of luck was I met Samantha Robinson who is now the mother of my baby son Beau and who will have become my wife by the time you read this. I already feel that she is, and we are working towards a strong future.

With the financial help of my brother, we have been

able to set up home together – and I've become an expert at DIY. I met Sam at a nightclub in 1999 and we hit it off. We started living together in 2000 and I've become a house-proud dad. Sam has been wonderful and 'little bug' Beau, he's been a godsend. He and my other kids helped get me through the prison system. Thank God, I am out of prison now and I've found happiness after all the bird I've been through. I feel lucky to have found someone like Sam and settled down – now I want to be a good family man. That's how I want to be. I've finished with crime and I now want to get on with my life. You might laugh at that switch of talents but, seriously, the pride in my home and my family saved me from spending the rest of my life behind bars.

For, in a twist of that Hollywood plot, it was the cozzers who tried to draw me back into the gangster world, who tried to prove that I was still an armed robber. I was still helping people out with problems, but there was never any way I wanted to take part in anything criminal.

If anything, after I got out from the Penthouse years I prevented crime and stopped violence. One night I got a call from a geezer who had got into bother with the wrong people. He shouted down the mobile: 'Vic, they're going to shoot my leg off.' When the geezers with the shotguns heard my name, they stopped the action. I was able to arrange a negotiation where they got the money they wanted and this mate of mine hung on to his left leg.

There were many times like that when I was able to cool

down situations; I had the respect and geezers knew that I would do what I said, that I was true to my word. My reputation was also priority insurance that there was no funny business from any of the people involved. I always had retribution as an option.

I still got four or five phone calls last week from people thinking I'm after them. I've had people begging me not to kill them – and I've never heard of them. When people hear my name and know what I am capable of, they tend to be nervous. Some bad boys use my name in vain, like you do with kids and the bogeyman. People are warned off with: 'If you don't behave we'll get Vic Dark after you.' That's why I'm sometimes called 'The Dark Man'. It's just to spook people. It doesn't do me any harm so I don't bother about it.

I have learned to be more live-and-let-live. Literally. I was brought up with the old values: letting grannies across the street and that. I've never robbed a working-class person in my life. I never will. I don't want it and I am not looking for trouble. Thank God my life has gone straight now. And I am glad for it – I've seen how it works on the streets and in prison in the 21st century.

What I have written about the prison system is as accurate as I can make it without dropping other people in the shit. I have lived the life of an armed robber and been tested and punished for it. There's not many people like me around today. Most people haven't grown up with that brutality of life.

I learned so much as an armed robber. The waiting game is hard. What makes people like me so dangerous is the willingness to go for it. Our targets in the old days never knew they were going to be taken out, there was no warning. When people talk about the executions of someone, it's only a certain breed of person who that could be.

That's what's made it so difficult for me to settle back into mainstream life. I carry my reputation with me. It's horrendous. I still find it difficult to allow someone to buy me a drink in a pub. I like to see the drink poured myself. It's old prison habits, worrying about the food and drink, concerned that the screws are doing more than pissing in it. It's hard to trust anyone. I read somewhere that all dangerous men are paranoid and it's the old joke: just because you think the bastards are after you doesn't mean they're not.

And the cozzers have become much more sophisticated. I am a free man but the authorities treat me in a terrorist category and use SAS standard equipment against me. I watch people from my house, 'repairmen' going up telephone poles or 'pensioners' walking their dogs. I know my telephone is tapped to fuck. If I get a new car, that'll be tapped up. They could be bugging me right now, just as I write these few words. Or looking at me. Cameras are so cheap nowadays – and devilishly good. I could sit here in my front room with no lights on and they could still look inside with an infrared camera. The technology is fantastic, so advanced. I've got to give respect to them. They are so fucking good now.

In the old days we had to be just as aware but we did not have the concerns of the hi-tech cameras and 'bugs' – or the closed-circuit telly cameras when you were doing a piece of heavy work. Then, the cozzers worked more with infiltrators, paid police informers. We had one on our firm. My mate was going out with her. Her name was Alex. We found out she was a police informer: it was the cozzers we knew who told us that! The slag worked as a manageress down at a club and she was telling the cozzers who was running drugs and what everyone was up to. She got paid a couple of hundred quid a week. She had a special code so that when she telephoned the cozzers they knew the information was proper. I don't know what happened to her. I never saw her around.

Of course the police have got a role to play. Of course they have. Let's get this right. I was not robbing the public. I was robbing the insurance companies, the security vans, the big sorting offices. It was the job of the blue hats to stop me doing that, one against the other. I knew the rules. And I learned more.

I had to switch off when I came out after the Penthouse jail time. I'm not going to say they won, but I would say that I had grown up. I'd learned. I'd learned that instead of wanting that car tomorrow I'd wait until I had the money for it. It took me three years to get my BMW. In my old game, if I wanted to have that BMW now, then I would have gone out to get the money for it. Now I can wait and do it properly, do it the straight way. My car's a couple of years old, not spanking new.

It might have taken me three years to get it, but it ain't cost me my liberty. It's like those blokes who drive around in big fucking motors, but you go round their houses and they're sitting on fucking orange boxes. The motor is all symbol, all flash. Lovely clothes and that and go round their house and it's like a fucking shithouse! But I wanted to get my house right first. Then I said, 'Right, I'll treat myself to a nice car.'

It's not a new car anyway, it's a couple of years old. I get a good deal on cars because I leave them parked on the dealers' showrooms. It's looked upon as a favour. Kids come along and see my car and say, 'Oh, Vic's car's on here,' and they leave the place alone. It's a little bit of protection. That's the sort of backhand type of thing that I get that helps me out. But it is all above board. I would never give the cozzers hope – they are very forward today and you can't give them an inch. They don't like me on the outside. They'd like me locked up and out of the way. But I have no intention of giving them any genuine reason to do that. I make a few bob these days by helping people out with their problems, by being a negotiator.

The other day I got a call from a geezer who had been cut up and he asked how much it would cost for me to sort the problem out. I went along to the people causing the trouble and said, 'Knock it on the head, the geezer's had enough.' I did not make any threats. I never do. I just delivered the message and happily they got it loud and clear. And I get paid for that. That's where I do a lot of money. Little firms fall out with each other or they want this or that done. As I explained, I've turned into a negotiator. And I have the track record to back it up. I can call on armies, and people know that.

Yet, my life has changed a lot. I remain too visible anyway to do anything. The police, they're not that stupid! I don't underestimate the police at all. It is not worth any amount of money for me to go back in jail. I've got too much to lose now. But I always did have my freedom to lose. So, why did I get into the armed robbery business? I have tried to explain it by writing about my background but, misguided as it certainly is, the very basic explanation is the power that violence gives you. No matter how you try to disguise it, that, I believe, is the truth of it. Because of my background, because of my need – and yes, greed – for things, I became a very violent man. And, in turn, a powerful one. It is intoxicating that power through violence that the Krays and other firms had.

I never wanted to advertise it – shout, 'Look at me, I'm cutting someone.' But it happened. I was fearless, and looking back at the banks and sorting offices we knocked over, it was well planned, well executed. We must have been doing it well or they wouldn't have set up special police squads to get us. It was very fast and effective and there was lots of money. There was also a lot of hurt but when you're younger you don't worry about that. You don't think it could mean years inside. I got a 12 when I was 21. What sort of life is that? I am trying to catch up with my life now. It's not easy.

I don't want to be one of those glamour gangsters with people wanting to shake your hand down the pub. I just want to get on with my life. I've retired but I've still got to go out and graft, not robberies or anything like that but you've got to earn a living.

There's a difference between the old school and the youngsters today – some of these young geezers would fucking nick the gold teeth out of your mouth. They'd break into your house and knock the old woman over for the watch on her hand. When I was 17, I thought that things were getting out of hand with football violence. People were getting fucking knifed and killed, stamped, glasses in their faces.

It's not for me to say who are the most terrible wrongdoers on earth. But I think it is all a matter of degree. Nonces are evil. Child killers should be locked up and stay away for the rest of their lives. Rapists? Well, what can I say about them? Obviously, they aren't as bad as child killers but, in my eyes, they are still bad people. The type of operators who are civilised are very on-the-ball and abide by their codes, which I've been brought up to do. You wouldn't see Joe Pyle or Roy Shaw fucking smashing a woman or anything like that.

People today terrify me. Who is dealing with the real evil? If someone attacks a bird and breaks her nose or rapes an old granny, you've got to deal with these people within your own society because the cozzers won't. You know someone who is bashing kids up? You've got to say don't to go to the police, talk to your uncle, or your dad and say: 'Look, he's fucking hitting her. She's only a kid. Deal with it.'

I think in today's society there is a place for the vigilante. I don't mean to do something criminal, but just to sort it out man to man.

What I have done is get into debt collecting – it is a weird business but it is a massive one. There is a lot of bankruptcy staged for people to get out of paying up. The main geezers have got the money but it's disguised in the paperwork, wrapped up in pen and ink where no one can find it. That's where I come in. I can deal easily with people who owe each other thousands of pounds but the harder ones involved millions.

They're the ones you really have to intimidate. I use the law. The perps know full well they've had people over; they know it. They know they've had the million pounds but they say there's nothing they can do about it. It's really, really sad because a lot of firms go under. They shrug and say that's that.

Of course, it's not that if I am called in.

They are very crafty and it can involve ten to fifteen

businesses going out all at once. One man has taken all the owners' livelihood off them and destroyed them. But it's legit and the geezer messing with people's lives knows every rule and it is hard sometimes to make it clear that he has done something wrong. What I do with a bankruptcy is I have the paperwork and a couple of associates – one's a professional boxer – with me; they stay in the background until I need them. If you go to the door three-handed, no one will open that door. I always dress smartly with a tie and shirt, and the door is usually opened straight away.

The code is I go and knock on the door and say, 'Excuse me, is Brian there?'

The woman says, 'Who are you?'

I say, 'A friend.'

She says, 'What's your name?'

I say, 'Steve.'

She's goes out and she shouts, 'Brian.'

I say to him, 'Are you Brian?'

He goes, 'Yeah.'

And as soon as he's shaken my hand that's the code for me to say this is Brian, the man we're after. If I don't shake your hand, then they don't come. It's a warning. Once I shake your hand, they are there. The usual thing I would say to them is 'Do you agree on this?' I give them a bit of paper with all the bankruptcy stuff on it and that. Some of them stand and some try to shut the door. If they shut the door then I kick the door in. Most of them don't say they owe

£37,000 – they admit they owe £32,000. I say, 'If you pay back £32,000, we'll clear that debt.' Some of them pay, some of them don't. Those that don't, they go to phone the police, then I step back out of it. Then I come back a few months later. Finally, they all understand that I *never* go away.

I don't do anything else. Sometimes if I'm doing private work, helping someone with a favour, it can get a little rough but never nasty enough to be illegal. I went to see one geezer whose father-in-law had loaned him 40 grand. I asked him if he agreed with it and he said, 'Yes', but that the father-in-law wasn't getting it and neither was I. He then tried to close the door and I put my foot in the door. He tried to hit me and it got a bit nasty then. But we all knew what it was about and it was private. There were no complaints and he paid the debt. Usually geezers owe the money because they've bought some puff and then don't pay for it. Most debts are paid off in instalments.

Out of 100 debts, two would go that way. There's not a lot of violence. A lot of people think debts are run on violence – they're not. When there is violence, I step out of it. The good thing with me is that I can choose what I do. I can pick. I also do favours for people wanting others to keep their mouths shut. It's just a matter of enforcing your point of view. I am very careful about what I do because the cozzers would love to have me back inside. They are as keen as mustard as you are about to find out. But I am happy getting my life back. I stay with Sam most of the time. I want to stay out of trouble but what do you do? I'm a likeable person. I've got no enemies. But …

Before Sam and I moved in together we were out one night and there was a call from her brother Danny – he's at a club and he says there are about 50 youngsters wanting to kill him. I jumped in the car and went down there. There's about 100 of them, all kids, about 17 or 18: a little firm had slipped in, hurt a few of them and fucked off. Danny has gone out for drink with a couple of birds he's pulled and now they want to kill him. There was a doorman holding this nasty mob back, but only just. They could have overpowered him at any moment if they'd wanted to have a go back in the club. When I got out of the car, there was me, the doorman and Danny and his mates. I'm a big lump and it was like back to the days of football violence. The mob didn't know what to do. They wanted to attack but they didn't have a direct leader to say 'Charge'. Because I was saying to a few mouthy ones, 'Come on then,' that was enough to intimidate them. That – and the way I looked.

I suppose I have that aura of serious intent. It certainly worked that night – and no violence on my part was involved.

My life is fairly complicated – I'm not some everyday geezer! My life is full of so many things. You won't meet many people who have been in as much aggro as me. That's not being big-headed or anything. I'm still young enough to turn it around.

Yet, I admit, I am still learning how to adapt to people,

to become part of society. At first, I didn't want to walk through the front door, and didn't want to do this or that and I didn't want to go out. My philosophy has changed. You do change as a person.

I haven't lost my asshole, but I know if I fuck up I will never be coming home again, and that fear factor alone is enough to keep me out of trouble. My life means much, much more to me now than ever before. Sam is like a breath of fresh air. I've got my baby, I've got Sam. These are my thoughts all the time. And that I don't want to be in another prison.

I have more solid ambition, different dreams.

And that made the nightmare all the more foreboding when it screeched back into my life.

That was on 16 February 2002, when a team of police roared up in cars and ambushed me. I was arrested at gunpoint and charged with conspiracy to commit armed robbery. The cozzers were armed with self-loading Smith and Wesson pistols and Heckler and Koch MP5s, nasty little machine pistols. All I had was a knife in my pocket – and a look of total dismay on my face. I was about to walk a tightrope of emotions for the next seven months. My future, my life, was to be put in the hands of strangers, a jury.

The cozzers had called their expensive campaign against me 'Operation Freeze'. It wasn't anything about hands-up-or-we'll-shoot.

The intention was to freeze-frame my life. Behind bars.

CHAPTER THIRTEEN

'OPERATION FREEZE'

'THEY SPENT NEARLY A MILLION
POUNDS TRYING TO PUT ME IN JAIL FOR
THE REST OF MY LIFE.'

VICTOR DARK, 2003

My life was in a good place at the beginning of 2002. I was working on this book, keeping up my karate training, helping with some youngsters at a fitness club and doing as much to my house as possible.

We were a happy, nuclear family, me and Sam, our son Beau and Sam's lovely six-year-old daughter Ellie. We had, like most families, developed a routine throughout the week which revolved around Ellie being taken to and from school, and me doing jobs around the house and working for my brother. My place was looking just how I wanted it and I was on a good, natural high.

The highlight at that moment was waiting for my new curtains to be delivered – not going on an armed robbery.

We are lucky that Sam's parents live nearby so we can

call on our babysitters, which we do mostly on Friday nights. That's when I liked to go out for a drink. I *am* the bear with a sore head on Saturday mornings and all my mates knew not to bother Vic on a Saturday morning.

That week ending on Saturday morning of 16 February 2002, I had spent four days grafting on the house. My hands were cut to bits with all the sawing and banging and painting I'd been up to. I was still doing a bit of ducking and diving: buying and selling tobacco which was safe and earned me a few bob. That week I had received a telephone call to say that a lorry was coming through with 25,000 sleeves of snout and did I want to buy some. They wanted £17.25 for a sleeve of 200 Bensons, and that's cheap. I was interested but, because they were so cheap, I wanted to see the cigarettes for myself before I bought them. There's a lot of dodgy snout around and I was only going to pay for the real thing. There's a lot of people out there who are happy to take the piss. I didn't want any of that. I wanted to have a look for myself – what a mistake!

First, I did not know that the National Crime Squad were out to get me. This lot, the British FBI, are a tooled-up lot. They are a heavy team.

Second, I did not know how paranoid my mate Dave Roberts had become about people breaking into his house.

Dave's place was in the middle of nowhere and he was asking for trouble. He kept getting robbed. He'd had all the Christmas presents stolen in one of four robberies and

I didn't realise how it was affecting him. It got so bad Dave called the police. Now that shocked me more than anything. His house was always going to get raided and I told him so. The gypsies would be after him. Dave just worried about it and he had trouble with his girlfriend she was scared to stay there.

I didn't find out until it was way too late that a mate of Dave's gave him a gun, as it turned out a Spanish piece known as the 'Firestar'. It's a 9mm pistol, a neat little thing. But what the fuck was Dave doing with it? Later, he told me he wanted to scare the gypsies off with it and he'd also got hold of a police warrant card which had belonged to a DC off Scotland Yard's Serious and Organised Crime Group. That bloke had 'lost' his card while attached to the National Crime Squad. Dave was going to wave the warrant card, like some crucifix keeping off the vampires, in the gypsies' faces too, as if they would have cared.

But Dave was out to protect his home no matter what. He bought a siren off another mate and picked up blue and green lights at a boot sale. His idea was to have his house light up and the siren to go off if it was raided.

It didn't matter. His girlfriend refused to go back no matter how much security he promised and had already arranged. Dave was in a mess, really heartbroken, because he had to move house. He got hold of a friend of ours, Lee Steward, and together they got a van and packed up a lot of Dave's stuff.

This is where I come into the picture – a right muggins in the frame, as it were. I need to get down to Bournemouth on Saturday to see and hopefully buy the snout on offer. I've fixed up the money and on the Friday night I telephoned Dave looking for a van to use.

So, on the Saturday morning, Dave and Lee turn up in the van. All I saw was a red Ford Transit. As far as I'm concerned, we're off to Bournemouth to see about the snout. The deal is being arranged by some guys I know from up north, from Manchester. We're going to get details on the mobile as we drive there. Lee drove the van; Dave and I went in a Vauxhall Omega estate.

I didn't want to go. I was tired, my hands were cut up from the decorating and I felt like shit. I wasn't sure about the snout. It was all a right pain but I thought I was going to profit well from just a day's work. If all went well.

It didn't.

Dave only had the fucking gun in his van. I didn't have a clue. Also in there with all his bags and personal belongings were the blue and green lights. I had never thought to ask what was in the van, why should I have? As far as I was concerned the van was to pick up the snout, end of story.

Somewhere along the line, Dave must have told someone close to him what was in the van. That someone grassed him, or us, up to the police. My quiet day out for a bit of business and quickly home for dinner with Sam and a couple of friends – we'd even booked the restaurant – went to hell.

The northern boys had been slow at getting out of bed. I could not get them on the mobile to guide us to the pick-up point. Then, later, after we did make contact, they still were not out of their hotel. They asked us to go and have a cup of tea and some breakfast and wait. We went off the M3 and into the Fleet service station. I went in and bought some phone cards and drinks – 'Red Bull' to help with the hangover – and then we went over to the canteen area.

There were people around us and we ordered a big English breakfast, the full Monty, and Dave needed something light to eat. He's had a heart attack so if he ate all that stuff he'd drop dead. Lee and I tucked in and I wanted to have a heart-to-heart with Lee about him leaving his girlfriend – who we're friendly with – for a younger woman. As I was talking to him I saw something out of the left side of my eye and there was this blonde bird staring at me. I thought, 'Does she fancy me? Nah,' but that gave me the inkling that something wasn't right.

I went outside and Dave was waiting for me. Lee got in the van and I got in the car with Dave. We were driving out of the service station through an isolated area when a car rolled in front of us. I thought it was some old boy who'd lost control of the car. We went straight into the side of it and because we smashed into it they had to leap out the other side of the car.

I thought I was a goner. I thought it was a set-up.

Then, all of a sudden I heard a shout: 'Police!' I thought, 'Thank God for that.'

There were hordes of them. They had on those baseball caps, the chequered ones with 'POLICE' spelled out so you'd notice. They'd had units follow us. When I realised what was going on, I spotted the unmarked cozzer cars. It was neatly done. They all had machine guns and some also had sidearms. They seemed to have come from everywhere, from off the motorway and out of the bushes. They might have been hanging off the trees like monkeys, there were so many of them.

I'd hardly copped all this when there were geezers all around the car. They put guns to either side of my head. I looked to the left and there were more police with machine guns. It was well set up for us. They told me: 'Get out of the car.' And then they ordered me to kneel down. There was some silly bastard running up and down with a flick cosh and I said to him, 'You fucking idiot.' I kept saying it to him and every time he went to hit me with it I said, 'You fucking idiot.'

They wouldn't come near me and then they asked, 'Are you armed?' I said, 'Yes. There's a knife in my left pocket.' Then they handcuffed me, took out the hunting knife – a lock-knife with a four-and-a-half-inch blade and five-inch handle – out and shunted me away and stood me against the wall. I had the knife with me because I always like a bit of protection but it was also there for a practical reason – to cut one of the sleeves of tobacco to make sure they were the Bensons. But the cozzers were not concerned about knives. They wanted to see some shooters about the place. At that point they thought Dave was me. He was surrounded by the cozzers with machine guns – it was like Custer's Last Stand. And then the blonde bird from the service station runs out and points at me shouting, 'That's the dangerous one.'

Whoever had lied to them that we were on a bit of work had said that I was the one with the gun driving the car. But I wasn't. That was Dave.

They were searching the van and to this day I really believe they tried to put a bullet in the chamber of the gun. They were in there too long to be doing anything else. I believed they were going to put a bullet in the gun from the ammunition clip of seven bullets. I really do believe that.

After that I told them nothing but the truth – that I was going to buy some tobacco. What happened that day was that I went out of my house, drove down the motorway, stopped at the petrol station, had a pee, bought a couple of Red Bull and headache pills, pulled out and got nicked.

My solicitor told me later that the reason they jumped me was that they didn't want to get me into an area where I could have got out with a gun. They were terrified there would be a big gun battle with me like before.

That's why they stopped us.

If they thought we were on an armed robbery they normally would have let us carry on and caught us in the act.

They didn't because they were frightened of me.

Yet, they must have thought we had three handguns or more with us. But we didn't have guns or masks or anything like that. Just that gun of Dave's which was there for a daft reason, nothing sinister. If I had been found in possession of a gun that would have been me forever – goodbye. The worst thing about it is that I didn't even know there was a gun in the van. I never thought about that.

Nevertheless, we were all charged with conspiracy to commit armed robbery – and I was off to prison again. This time they had me on remand at HMP Highdown in Sutton, Surrey. I had never wanted to go into the dungeons of the British prison system again but here I was – and an innocent man. I don't think I've ever been so fucking angry. And then I didn't know that the Government was willing to spend nearly one million pounds to send me back to jail. And keep me there.

Highdown Prison was hell all over again. And I wasn't alone in there. Mostly, I was banged up 23 hours a day. It was a liberty-taking place. There was a con in there, Dave Orrin, who had been there for 22 years. He got a home leave and was a couple of hours late getting back. While he was out on leave there was a robbery. He got the blame and he was never near the place. He'll be inside forever. There was another one, Trevor Hicks; his girlfriend said he was a serious danger to women so, on her word and after 15 years, they kept him locked up. It's the easier option.

They don't have humanity. They don't know the meaning of the word.

Highdown is a bad place. We had a TV, but the attitude of the screws was terrible. One talked to me in a way that was typical of them. He said, 'Some dickhead up there cut himself. He ain't done a good job, he's still alive.' That's how they look upon it and it is a horrible way to be. The next morning when I got up, another con had taken an overdose, the barbarity of the treatment and the views of the screws had finally been too much for him. I can't believe I'm saying this but they don't have enough screws, which is part of the pressure in the whole prison system, but that should not turn them into complete arseholes. They've got no screws, they are short of staff, and that meant we got nothing. I was on remand yet I couldn't go the gym. I was locked up most of every day, like everybody else.

I was living on bread and butter. We got one of those tiny packets of cornflakes and a sachet of jam about 8am and that did you until 1pm. They allocate more to feed a dog a day than they spend on people in prison, which is £1.25. I got a little bit more because they were like that with me. Yet when they didn't know who I was they were stroppy. As soon as they knew I was Victor Dark, their backs went up but they knew they couldn't treat me like a knobby.

I was caged in an 'A' van on the way to a court appearance and some screw is sitting there and sees all the cops and says to me, 'All this for a pair of mugs.' I just looked at him.

When they prepared me to leave the cage they handcuffed me – twice. They double-cuffed me. As I stood up and walked out I looked at this screw and said, 'You think I'm a mug, do yah?' The other screws were going, 'Leave it out Vic, leave it out.' He was only a young screw. When I was in the cage this screw was all blow and wind – out of it I was a different beast, even handcuffed, and he was intimidated by me. He shit himself, saying, 'I didn't mean it. I didn't mean it.'

The Security Officer (SO) turned to me and said, 'Thanks for not knocking him out. He deserved it.'

I went through nervy weeks of being taken to and from court. I was touted as the Most Wanted Man in Britain – and the screws treated me that way. Every moment I spent out of a prison cell I was under guard, handcuffed, in a cage, in a van, and sometimes both. There were armed police when I was transported – they treated me as if was Hannibal Lecter. And there were times when I'd have loved to chew them up. Yet I knew I had to be cool and let the hand play itself out. I knew I was not going on a robbery. All the evidence was circumstantial.

But, a big but, there was always doubt. And wouldn't it have been ironic if I'd been locked away for the rest of my life just for trying to make a few bob on a bit of tobacco? Crazier things have happened in the legal system.

With my background, the cozzers were convinced I was guilty. What about a jury? I had to narrow the odds.

I was not confident with the solicitor I had. I felt I could do better and I was told that the best in the country was a lawyer called David Turner of south London. It was the best move I ever made. Saved my life. David Turner brought in the barrister Dermot Wright and his colleague Charlie Benson. What a fantastic legal team. Knights in shining armour. They saw the whole story and what a set-up it was.

Of course, Dermot still had to convince a jury who had been selected randomly, turning our future into a real lottery. Dave and Lee had different counsel but, finally, we all went on trial together at Winchester Crown Court in August 2002.

What a performance it was to be in the town founded by King Alfred the Great. Historic? It could have been for me. If it had gone wrong I might as well have had my head cut off. Or been hung, drawn and quartered. The court is in a set of modern buildings near the Great Hall and Round Table. I wasn't expecting any chivalry.

I was taken from Highdown in an armoured police van. There was a police escort. Station wagons at the front and rear of the van. The cozzers in the cars had automatic weapons trained on the van for the trip to and from court.

Sam was in Winchester for the trial and she told me I was like an alarm call for the city – they could hear me from miles away: sirens were blaring and helicopters were trailing us, noisy vultures in the sky. It was presidential, this security. I could hear the fanfare myself as the sirens played us into Winchester city centre.

The lawyers told me about the rest – the armed police surrounding the court building. There were cozzers armed with Heckler and Koch MP5 carbines: they are 9mm extending stock, single shot, three burst weapons. This armed team of cozzers was all around the courthouse and the court itself. Sam and others had to go through a security point, like they have at airports. Then everyone going into the court was frisked at the entrance by one of about half-a-dozen uniformed cozzers. Most of the 'spectators' in the court as well as 'reporters' in the press box were actually members of the National Crime Squad. Sam says one of her friends thought I'd shot the Queen and tried to run off to Rio with the Crown Jewels. It was that sort of security. People around the courts had never seen anything like it.

Then I heard the worst news of all. The jury were going to be 'protected' – they were going to have an armed guard on them and their homes for the duration of the trial. Now what were they going to think? What was Regina vs Victor

Dark, David Roberts and Lee Steward *really* all about? I knew I had a chance of getting out of it for the case was all based on paper. But a protected jury? I thought with a protected jury I was gone. There had only been one person I'd known who got out of a protected jury and that was Kenny Noye.

No matter what the jury were told, I felt they had to think there was something really going on here. Conspiracy to armed robbery? If I was a juror I'd have to think there was more to it than that. Why else would an armed cozzer be at my house all the time?

My concerns didn't help my health. I'd lost a lot of weight in prison – I was paranoid about what I was eating. I feared anything could happen to me at this stage of the game, for what an absurd one it was.

My clothes were hanging off me the day we got to court and that didn't help my confidence. Dermot questioned the judge about the police being all over the place and the need for a protected jury. The judge went all out to be fair during the trial but he was not giving an inch on the security. He told the court that he had been given 'genuine and compelling' evidence that there was a 'serious danger' of an attempt to 'nobble' the jury. It was funny to hear him say that word: nobble. Well, I suppose judges get pulled into the parlance just like we do.

The extraordinary police presence was again, said the judge, because of information received that there was to be an 'attempt to leave custody'. He stressed that he knew the difference between true information and 'tittle tattle'. He'd been told I was going to try and blow the gaff, make The Great Escape. The way they had me guarded I'd have needed an army of tanks to get out.

I didn't know anything about any of it. I had to sit in the dock between Dave and Lee and listen and take it. I was in the hands of the jury – and Dermot and Charlie Benson. What I did know was that the cozzers had tried to get my mates to put in the word against me. They approached Dave Roberts a week before the trial and said, 'Give us something on Vic Dark, and we'll just give you a year.' They did that to lots of people, trying to pump up a case they didn't have against me. It was unbelievable. They tried everything they could to get me. Dave would have got a year, but they would have put me away for life.

For nothing. The prosecution did not know who we were going to rob. They couldn't. There wasn't going to be a robbery. But they argued that because of how we were dressed – we had suits on to make the point to the tobacco lot that we were serious people – and with the lights and gun in the van that we were on a heavy piece of work.

When the cozzers questioned us they implied we were disguised as policemen – we had the suits, a warrant card and what they said was a police klaxon as well as the lights in the back of the van. I think Mike Yarwood would have given a better impression of a cozzer than we did. It was total bollocks.

A lot of their case hinged on whether my thumbprint was on that warrant card and I do believe it was and that the cozzers put it there. It was 'lifted' off something else and put on the card. Dermot really went after that in court. I knew it was something in our favour. In Highdown, I met this Egyptian, Barry. He was the nice fella in the Taliban I mentioned before. He had been a barrister for the Taliban for 15 years. He'd been locked up as a terrorist and had been in prison for three years. I showed him the paperwork for my case and he focused on the warrant card.

As it turned out, the warrant card had been taken out of an evidence packet. Anybody could have tampered with it. The sealed numbers on the packet were wrong. The judge sensed that something was amiss. Dermot and Charlie Benson were fantastic. They went for it and Dermot just made the cozzers and the prosecution look silly. But he did it in his lovely, quiet, legal way, making the point clearly, spelling it out for the jury that all they were hearing was circumstantial evidence.

Nevertheless, sitting in the dock, there was a lot to be concerned about. The trial went on day after day and even got the attention of the High Sheriff of Hampshire who sat on the bench to listen in on proceedings.

And each morning and evening the procedure was the same: armed police, caged in a van, helicopters buzzing in the sky above Winchester, and me on my way back to prison. My nightmare was that one day they'd take me back to prison and the key would just be lost. I would be in a cage forever. After all that had happened and my good intentions to settle into a family life, it was a horror story rattling around in my head. But I had to stay as cool as possible. Dermot and Charlie came to see me each day and we went over what had happened in court.

I knew Sam and some of my friends waited outside court for the armoured van to leave with me. I heard her shouting, 'Vic! Vic!' and I always gave a great noisy thump to the side of the van just to let her know, to let them all know, that I was alive and kicking and not giving into all the shit being chucked at me.

CHAPTER FOURTEEN

DEFROSTED

'MY HOUSE HAS TO BE LIKE A FORTRESS.'

VICTOR DARK, 2003

'Good luck, Vic, we're with you,' read one of the cards I got at Highdown. There were scores of them wishing me well. And letters from people I hadn't seen or heard from for years. People who know the game, how it works, knew I'd been set up. But, like me, they didn't have a clue what the outcome would be.

But I had a cheerleading team – and the BBC, unknowingly, on my side.

My brother Tony's company, UK Packaging, sponsors the boxer Dominic Negus. Now Dominic is a great boxer – and he's a good friend too.

He had a fight against Audley Harrison in July 2002, while I was still kicking my heels in Highdown. It was at the Wembley Conference Centre in London and Dominic and some of his supporters got white T-shirts printed up with 'VIC DARK IS AN INNOCENT MAN' on them.

The fight was being televised and when the producers saw the T-shirts they went apeshit. The BBC! There was to be no publicity and they banned Dominic and the others from wearing the shirts in front of the cameras. They got the security staff to make them take their T-shirts off. But, when they shouted out for Dominic to go into the ring they put the T-shirts back on and marched straight past the security. They just walked through them without a whimper or a problem. There was about five of them. The security men didn't know what to do – as it turned out it would have been a better fight than the one that happened in the ring.

When Dominic was in the ring, where he was walking around, the BBC cameras kept off the shirt, all you could see was his boxing gloves. But they couldn't avoid it forever. At one point the camera caught 'VIC DARK IS AN INNOCENT MAN'. Dominic put his arms in the air and you could see it clear as a bell.

We had the fight on the telly in Highdown and when that clip went on there was a great cheer and lots of thumping and banging. It was terrific publicity for me for it got my case out there.

Sadly, Audley Harrison defeated Dominic on points but either of them could have been disqualified. I think all the fuss about me at the beginning of the fight didn't help.

Dominic is a small geezer and in the fourth round Harrison stunned him with a well-timed cross.

Dominic took an arsehole of a hit. He turned his head, knelt and rested his arm on the middle rope but did not place a hand or knee on the canvas. Harrison was perfectly entitled to hit Dominic again and he did.

All the Essex boys were there to support one of their own and there were shouts of outrage. But Dominic was angrier than any of the crowd of 2,000. He chased Harrison across the ring and whacked him ever so well with a headbutt. Now, of course, in boxing that's against the rules.

Harrison, who won at the Sydney Olympics, earned it though – he was guilty of several low blows during the six rounds. Dominic, who was a cruiserweight, tried. He landed some good punches and in the fifth round I thought he might take it for Harrison ran out of steam; he was really wheezed. He got his second wind in the sixth round and that was it for Dominic.

He may have lost (59–55 scorecard) that night but he made it a victory for me.

I had a lot of support in the build-up to the trial and during it. But the tension took its toll: back and forward from court to prison; watching the jury and wondering what they were *really* thinking. Did they know my past history? Had someone sneaked that information to them? Would they want me banged up for ever and ever? But Dermot and Charlie Benson thought we had a good case;

the prosecution had no case, for the simple reason that there wasn't one.

I spent a lot of time thinking about my life during this period. What it came down to was that I had lived my life, participated in it, but I hadn't been in charge of it. Now I so wanted that control. As a free man.

I was found not guilty of conspiracy to commit armed robbery. I was given a year's sentence for possession of the hunting knife. Dave had admitted possession of the handgun and got three years. Lee was found not guilty and walked free. Winchester Crown Court suddenly became the most perfect place in the world that day. I was going home. Thanks to Dermot. Love him! A brilliant man.

The faces on the cozzers! They looked pale and as if they were about to throw up. Some of the National Crime Squad geezers who had sat in plain clothes during the trial turned up for the verdict in uniform. They looked sick as dogs.

The jury looked a little shocked too when the court clerk read out my previous convictions. One woman looked as though she was going to burst out crying. I can't blame her – my convictions are, literally, as long as my arm. And I've got big arms. I felt like crying myself, I was so happy. Justice!

Dermot told the judge that if I was given an extra three months on the time I had already served on remand that would give me nine months and I could be released from custody. The judge wasn't having any of that! He said I would be sentenced to a year. He thought I would spend three more months in prison.

Dermot, I have to give him his due, led him right into it. What the judge forgot was you get half time and out. I had already done my share of that sentence but the judge didn't realise I would be released. Dermot was brilliant. I owe so much to that guy. He saved my life. I can't ever thank him enough – and that good man Charlie Benson.

Of course, I was now a big problem for the prison service. They had to free a high-risk 'Cat AA' prisoner. The Governor at Highdown apparently shit himself. Not many people have been let out at that risk level. The Governor didn't know what to do. There were phone calls flying back and forth.

I had to go back from Winchester to Highdown but I was a free man. Well, the security was heavier than ever. If I had been found guilty, they were ready for me to make a break for it. There were armed cozzers all over the place, sharpshooters in the escort cars and me in the cage in the armoured van.

A free man?

Not quite yet.

The Security Officer (SO) from Highdown was on the blower to the Governor – still shitting himself, according to the SO – and I asked him: 'What did the Governor say?'

The SO said, 'He said, "Fuck me."'

They didn't let me out of Highdown until 2.30pm the next day. Sam was waiting for me and had been hanging about for hours. Some screw had been abrupt with her, telling her she'd have to wait.

They walked me out of Highdown – now, I've been found not guilty – with three dog handlers as part of the guard.

Sam is out there doing her nut. When I was coming through security at the gates the screw said to me, 'I didn't mean to be rude to your girlfriend.' I didn't know what the geezer was talking about. Of course, I was a different proposition for them now. I was a free man. Their attitude went from arrogant to compliant. I was back on the streets. That is where my power is – on the street, because I know everyone.

I went home a 'Cat AA'.

POSTSCRIPT:
IN FROM THE COLD

'THANK GOD FOR WHAT'S HAPPENED TO ME
NOW. I'VE MET SAM. I'VE GOT THE KIDS. THAT
WAS MY DREAM. SHE'S GOT ME THROUGH IT,
AND THIS IS WHAT I WANTED TO HAVE AND
THAT'S THE END OF THE STORY.'
VICTOR DARK, 2003

It's impossible for me to fully explain the feelings when you step outside of prison and breathe the air as a free man. Somehow, it tastes different, it makes your lungs expand so much better. You take a deep breath and it's never a sigh, it's a delight, a celebration.

I don't want to get all maudlin, but for those seven months inside for no reason – I'd cope with hell if it was my due – I felt absolute frustration, a spinning of wheels, for there was nothing I could do to prove my case. How do you prove a negative? How do you prove you didn't do something that didn't happen? I had to leave all that work to others.

When they reluctantly allowed me to leave Highdown a screw said to me, 'I suppose you owe a big thank you to

God.' He was being seriously sarcastic. He grinned with that sort of sickly smile, as though he'd just vomited. I shocked him when I said, 'Yeah, I do.' I told him I slept with the Bible under my pillow. If anyone has been helped it has been me.

I am not religious – and I really know it sounds crap – but at the time I was sentimental about it. I had nothing else to hold on to. I suppose that is how faith begins. I was fighting for my life. With the Bible under my pillow I did sleep. It's like some mystical dream now, but at the time …

I had come out of prison and started a new life with Sam and with Beau. I have a good lifestyle. We all love each other.

And someone wanted to end that, to put me away. I was at the end of a chain and they thought they could yank it, could choke me, could end life as I wanted it. One of four people put me there. Someone knew I was on the end of that chain. He was really cocksure.

It was a bit of a shock when I got off. But I wasn't going on an armed robbery. I'd done nothing. Seven months for nothing. It was a frightening experience. I was numb to it, but I could have got life. I wasn't in the bad way that I thought I would be. I tried to be a bit of a gladiator about it. Even waiting for the verdict.

I was sweaty-palms as you'd expect, but I didn't feel that my life was going to end. It was weird. Looking in the back of my mind, I knew I had a good chance of going home. I needed a bit of strength and I know I keep going back to this Bible crap but it was true. That Bible sort of protected me. I had this protection around me. It was really weird. If they believed that I was really guilty and I had a nasty mind, do you think I'd have got a not guilty? I think all the powers and all the prayers and everything from my family and everyone around me got me home. It choked me up.

One of the cozzers, a Scottish geezer who was a bit thick, turned to me at the Fleet service station and said, 'I'm surprised you're on this, Vic.' I wondered how he knew my name and how he was surprised I was on something I wasn't on. I see that they really tried to put me away. It was all set up for me. They were so sure they had me nicked. These sort of things make me smile now.

Well, fuck 'em. Fuck 'em all. That's my motto.

It might not be God's, but between us we won.

I am now in charge of my life and I will dictate what happens, which is something – if you don't break the law – that every man deserves. Money is important for giving my family a good lifestyle but it is no longer important enough for me to want to steal it.

That, of course, won't keep the cozzers happy. After you come out a high-risk prisoner you have to take precautions. I truly believed they would try to fit me up again.

And they did. In October 2002, not that long after that nonsense in Winchester. I had gone to a boot sale in Hackney Marshes with the boxer Dominic Negus and a couple of our mates. I bought a couple of CDs, a bobble hat for Beau and a couple of other bits and pieces.

On the drive back, on the A12 one of the guys, Trevor, says, 'Look, there's a helicopter up there. And there's a police car, and another police car ...' All of a sudden, about five or six of the cozzer cars block off the road. There are a couple of choppers buzzing around above us. It's on the A12 near Wanstead station and the cozzers are mob-handed with machine guns. They took us all out of the car and off to the side of the road.

It was the spread-the-legs treatment, and they searched the car. They took us off to Ilford police station and I was there for about five hours. There was a little knife found in the glove compartment and they tried to say it was mine, but Trevor put his hands up. He's a florist and he uses the knife in his work, and that was it.

They had to let us go. They said they searched us because a member of the public had said there was a gun in the car. And that, of course, was a load of old bollocks. They had to release me. But it was nice in a way. I was able to cunt them up and get away with it.

It's not a nice way to live but that's the way it is. I've cast myself as the gamekeeper now. The cozzers are the poachers. What worries me, and I hope I am being paranoid, is that they will break into my house and plant stuff – probably drugs which I have never, never dealt with – that could get me back in court. I have bought a security system for the house with cameras and the rest, if not stop them, then to catch them in the act.

I have to make my house like a fortress. I will change my car every couple of weeks through my car dealer mates, because the cars will be targets too. I have a device to tell if my phone is being bugged. I was talking to a friend the other day and although I'm his mate I still don't trust him. I asked him to lift his jacket and T-shirt. The cozzers are smart people, they're good, they're very good, and they can get to people. They are dealing with the terrorism out in Ireland. The National Crime Squad (NCS) have got unlimited funds and I have had vans outside the house: people keep looking in.

I either have to move abroad or get security. I don't fancy a Spanish fry-up. My stuff is top-of-the-range anti-surveillance but, of course, the cozzers have got top-of-the-range surveillance. It's a Mexican stand-off.

What an irony! After all these years of blagging, of blasting into banks and other places I'm the one working to keep people out now. When it comes to my home I am still an extremely hard bastard and I want everyone to know that. I have different ambitions now but the main one is to protect those I love.

That makes me more dangerous than ever.

I've told you all about my antics, my adventures, but with all honesty, I have to say that the last pull, for the non-existent conspiracy in an armed robbery, was the worst of all experiences. Yet it taught me something. I'm not invincible. I'm not as clever as I thought I was. I let my guard drop and I know I let an informer into my life. A bad one and all.

I am on the streets now and a lot of people are safer. If I wasn't around lots of my mates might be dead.

I am an equaliser. Without me around to stop some of the aggravation, people will get killed. I'm like a guardian angel. As soon as I got out people got in touch with me.

Yet, now, I would never risk my liberty. Unless, as I indicated, it was to protect my family and my friends.

And, for all that has happened, I still retain my rule of no mercy for those who do me wrong. My oath now is to avoid situations where it will be an issue. I never ever want it to happen, but if it does I will still not ask for mercy. Or give it. I know if they ever lock me up again they will bury me and the key.

But they'll have to walk over a lot of bodies to get me.

You can unbuckle your seat belt now.

EPILOGUE:
LESSONS

'THE PRISON SYSTEM IS A CLASSROOM.'
VICTOR DARK, 2003

I've done my porridge. Now I'd like to say some things about the prison system which I hope might save a few lives. The first thing the Government has to do is get the bullying and the drug-taking in Young Offenders Institutions under control. All the cells have to be redesigned, the light fittings changed, the windows remodelled, to stop cons finding it so easy to hang themselves.

I think there should be an outside body, an organisation separate from the prison system, which has a helpline for prisoners who have been beaten or are cracking up or simply want to talk to someone. They should be given a card with a telephone number for a hotline.

Locking people up for 23 hours a day is doing no good

for cons or for society. What has to be introduced, especially for the youngsters, is a work training programme. Cons should be taught how to do a proper job, how to take pride in it. Now, all they do is lock the door on you.

Prisoners should be kept as close to home as possible for family visits. An outside body should also help with family problems, like allowing cons to have access to their children. I know that if there is a family unit you are far more likely to settle back into life in the straight world.

People coming out of prison need special counselling and help with getting back into society – money is always the big problem. If they don't have the money they're just going to steal it and there you go again, Catch-22.

Every lifer when he reaches his tariff should have a specialist organisation review his case and not leave him open to the threat – by any malicious individual – of an allegation which will keep him in or return him to prison.

More visits – contact with the outside world, people to talk to – should be encouraged.

My parting shot is to those taking heroin. I think all heroin dealers should be taken off the face of the earth. But to those hooked on it I say, 'It's not just you but your family that suffers.' I'm going through it with a young girl right now who is the daughter of a friend and it is a plague. I'd like to stamp out all the heroin out there.

I'd like all young people to get back to the old principles:

help people older than yourselves, don't grass on your friends, stick by the old school beliefs.

Finally, I think Britain and America should keep out of other people's troubles. It's nothing to do with us.

I think we should all be for Britain.

ACKNOWLEDGEMENTS

I'd like to thank my mum and dad who brought me into this world for everything they've done for me over my life, and also for my brother Tony. I'd also like to thank Sam's family, Rod Maynard and Jen, Mickey Robinson, Carol and Lauren, Sam and Viv, and the rest of the clan. It hasn't been easy for them as I've been in prison such a long time. Respect to Gavin Silver, Dave Roberts, Dominic Negus, Paul Cooper, Dave Rowlinson, Ray Coleman and Sarah, Gary Downey, Big Frank and The Baker, A.J., Joey Pyle, Roy Shaw, Freddie Foreman, Tony Lambrianou, all the Old Guard, and Kate Kray and Leo. Also to Sally Ansell, Les and John, Robert Pasqu and Dean. And to my friends in South London and Basildon, the two Foxes, Robert and John, little Lennie, the two Terrys, father and son, and Tony Baloney.

To all those in my life who've been in jail – especially for all the people who stood up to the prison system, Kevin B., Perry T. and all the other solid and staunch men I met like Warren Slaney and Charlie Bronson: keep your chin up, all respect.

I'd like to thank Dermot Wright, Charlie Benson and David Turner for being a brilliant legal team. Also John Blake and Douglas Thompson for giving me a chance with the book.

I owe so much to and am grateful to Sam for her strength and support, and a big thanks to her family. All my love to her and to my children, Megan, Jordan, Beau, Luke and Ellë.

As you've seen, this book is dedicated to all of you and to others whose names I'd best keep to myself.

God bless.

Vic Dark, 2006